FACULTY DEVELOPMENT IN THE AGE OF EVIDENCE

FACULTY DEVELOPMENT IN THE AGE OF EVIDENCE

Current Practices, Future Imperatives

Andrea L. Beach, Mary Deane Sorcinelli, Ann E. Austin, and Jaclyn K. Rivard

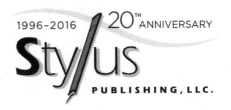

1996-2016 20TH ANNIVERSARY

Stylus

PUBLISHING, LLC.

STERLING, VIRGINIA

COPYRIGHT © 2016 BY
STYLUS PUBLISHING, LLC.

Published by Stylus Publishing, LLC.
22883 Quicksilver Drive
Sterling, Virginia 20166-2102

Library of Congress Cataloging-in-Publication Data
Names: Beach, Andrea L., author. |
Sorcinelli, Mary Deane, author. |
Austin, Ann E., author. | Rivard, Jaclyn K., author.
Title: Faculty development in the age of evidence :
current practices, future imperatives / Andrea L. Beach,
Mary Deane Sorcinelli, Ann E. Austin, and Jaclyn K. Rivard.
Description: Sterling, Virginia : Stylus Publishing, LLC, 2016. |
Includes bibliographical references and index.
Identifiers: LCCN 2016016629 (print) |
LCCN 2016030732 (ebook) |
 ISBN 9781620362679 (cloth : alk. paper) |
 ISBN 9781620362686 (pbk. : alk. paper) |
 ISBN 9781620362693 (library networkable e-edition) |
 ISBN 9781620362709 (consumer e-edition)
Subjects: LCSH: Universities and colleges--Faculty. |
College teachers--In-service training. |
College teachers--Professional relationships.
Classification: LCC LB2331.7 .B43 2016 (print) |
LCC LB2331.7 (ebook) | DDC 378.1/2--dc23
LC record available at https://lccn.loc.gov/2016016629

13-digit ISBN: 978-1-62036-267-9 (cloth)
13-digit ISBN: 978-1-62036-268-6 (paperback)
13-digit ISBN: 978-1-62036-269-3 (library networkable e-edition)
13-digit ISBN: 978-1-62036-270-9 (consumer e-edition)

Printed in the United States of America

All first editions printed on acid-free paper
that meets the American National Standards Institute
Z39-48 Standard.

Bulk Purchases

Quantity discounts are available for use in workshops and for
staff development.
Call 1-800-232-0223

First Edition, 2016

10   9   8   7   6   5   4

We dedicate this book to our colleagues in the Professional and Organizational Development Network in Higher Education and beyond it, whose commitment and efforts created the field of faculty development, and to those whose vision and passion will create its future.

CONTENTS

TABLES

INTRODUCTION

*O*pportunity and options, concern and constraint—these phrases could be used simultaneously to describe American higher education in the early decades of the twenty-first century. The changes and challenges facing universities and colleges are of intense interest to students, parents, legislators, and employers, and especially to the faculty members who carry out the missions of higher education institutions in teaching, research, and service. The creativity, dedication, and expertise faculty members bring to each part of their work are essential ingredients in the quality contributions universities and colleges make to their students and the broader society. Faculty members are supported in that work by institutional investments in professional faculty development that have strategic importance to the success of universities and colleges and to the professional accomplishments and personal well-being of the faculty. Examining faculty development today—its purposes, the roles of developers, key priorities, and new directions—is the topic of this volume.

Creating the Future of Faculty Development: Learning From the Past, Understanding the Present (Sorcinelli, Austin, Eddy, & Beach, 2006) was the first large-scale study of faculty developers in North America and Canada. The book presented a description of the evolution of faculty development, a portrait of developers and programs, an analysis of issues being addressed by faculty development services, and a summary of developers' views on priorities and future directions for the field. Recognizing that the context affecting higher education institutions and their faculty continues to change rapidly, this new book, *Faculty Development in the Age of Evidence: Current Practices, Future Imperatives*, takes a look at the field a decade after the earlier data were published. We were particularly interested in tracking the latest developments in the field and identifying new and emerging priorities and practices. We also witnessed mounting evidence that faculty development has become a more essential support for institutional strategic initiatives, a shift that offers opportunities and challenges to faculty developers and to faculty development centers (Austin, 2011; Cook & Kaplan, 2011; Maxey & Kezar, 2015; Schroeder & Associates, 2010). Our own and others' observations, research, and experiences encouraged our renewed examination of the current state of faculty development and the issues developers will be called on to address in upcoming decades.

As suggested by the title of our earlier book, understanding the state of affairs in faculty development and looking toward the next steps in an agenda for the future requires learning from the past and understanding the present. Thus, this introduction begins with an update on the discussion about the name and definition of the field, followed by a brief overview of the history or ages of faculty development, which was presented more extensively in the earlier volume. We then turn to the latest period, characterized as the Age of the Network, launched at the turn of the twenty-first century. Here we highlight the key issues that have had a significant effect on the field over the past decade or so. We also provide a recap for readers of the emerging agenda and critical questions we posed at the end of our earlier book, issues that we hoped would be in the forefront as faculty, academic leaders, and faculty developers planned for the future. We highlight the present-day landscape in higher education and current realities facing the field of faculty development and conclude with an overview of the book's organization.

The Definition of *Faculty Development* Revisited

Faculty development is not a new phenomenon in higher education, but as a profession it is young, having existed for less than half a century. Because it is a relatively new field, those of us in the profession still seek agreement on a name. Currently, the field of faculty development is referred to by a number of interchangeable terms, especially outside the United States, including *educational development, faculty development, staff development*, and *professional development*. Several scholars in the field note that the conversation about what to call the field remains productive but has not achieved consensus (Gillespie & Robertson, 2010; Schroeder & Associates, 2010; Sorcinelli et al., 2006). Readers may know the field by a number of terms; however, for consistency, we will continue to use *faculty development*, which is still a commonly accepted term, especially in higher education in the United States.

The seminal frameworks outlined by Bergquist and Phillips (1975) and Gaff (1975) were the earliest attempts to define the field. Bergquist and Phillips suggested that effective faculty development is multifaceted and put into practice across three dimensions: instructional, personal, and organizational development. Within this framework, developers focused on the improvement of college teaching and learning, the personal development of faculty (e.g., career planning), and a supportive and effective institutional environment for teaching and learning. They offered a broad and holistic view of faculty development. Nelsen (1981) described faculty development as "those activities designed to improve faculty performance in all aspects of professional lives—as instructors, scholars, advisors, academic leaders and contributors to institutional decisions" (p. 9). While acknowledging the importance of inclusivity in the definition of *faculty development*, others envisioned a tighter focus on teaching development and renewal. Gaff (1975), for example, defined it as "enhancing the talents, expanding the interests, improving the competence, and otherwise facilitating the professional and personal growth of faculty members, particularly in their role as instructors" (p. 14).

This tension remains active some 40 years later. As the field of faculty development has evolved, its programs span a continuum from one-on-one consultation on classroom instruction to programs for mentoring, scholarly writing, career advancement, leadership, and work-life balance. Some developers continue to make the case for an emphasis on supporting faculty in their roles as teachers and on assisting in the reform of undergraduate teaching and learning. Others argue that greater attention to the synergies among teaching, scholarship, institutional and professional citizenship, faculty relationships with colleagues and other members of the campus community, and the formation of leadership capabilities (Debowski, 2011; Schroeder & Associates, 2010; Sorcinelli, Gray, & Birch, 2011). Lee (2010) thoughtfully reflects that extending the reach of faculty development "constitutes equal parts opportunity and peril: the embrace of teaching and learning as a legitimate sphere of faculty concern and activity or the eclipse of teaching and learning by the dominant sphere of research" (p. 32). We suspect the tug and pull between greater focus and greater inclusivity in goals, structures, and services will continue to be the subject of ongoing and careful reflection in the incredibly varied faculty development programs, centers, colleges, and universities in the United States.

Similarly, the preeminent association of faculty developers, the Professional and Organizational Development (POD) Network in Higher Education, has grappled with this issue of professional identity since its founding in 1976. At its outset, its stated purpose was to provide a conceptual framework and maintain a network for supporting improvement in higher education through faculty, instructional, and institutional/organizational development (Buhl & Wilson, 1984). Given the centrality of faculty members to the work of teaching centers, the term *faculty development* encompassed the agendas of most programs, becoming the term predominantly used in the field and by the POD Network (and, to a large degree, this remains true today).

Much like any organization, however, its guiding principles and mission have evolved from its inception to the present day. In the POD Network's (n.d.) strategic plan (2013–2018), the *network* is defined as "an association of higher education professionals dedicated to enhancing teaching and learning by supporting educational developers and leaders in higher education" (para. 1), whose mission "encourages the advocacy of the on-going enhancement of teaching and learning through faculty and organizational development" (para. 2). Two terms in this updated definition of the field and its mission are worthy of note. First, current faculty development leaders in the POD Network have proposed that *educational development*, more common in Australia and Europe, might be a better frame for the field, encompassing work across disciplines, institutional levels, and areas such as student development, faculty development, and organizational leadership (Little, 2014). Second, the definition also delineates a movement toward a closer focus on *teaching and learning* rather than a broader range of faculty concerns. This may reflect a need by leaders to place some boundaries and borders on the field so that faculty development can meet the increasing expectations set for it by a range of stakeholders. As the research findings reported in this book suggest, however, faculty developers vary in the breadth of the purposes they see themselves responsible for addressing, and some of this variation likely relates to the needs of the faculty members they serve, the missions of the institutions where they work, and the external forces—the changing conditions of knowledge, technology, learning, and work—that press on higher education.

The Evolution of Faculty Development Revisited

In our original study, we conceptualized, divided, and described the historical development of the field into four ages (Age of the Scholar, Age of the Teacher, Age of the Developer, and Age of the Learner), which captured the evolution of faculty development over the past half century. We further argued that the field was entering a new age, that of the Age of the Network. We further want to note that although earlier ages were focused on specific people and their roles (i.e., scholar, teacher), this latest age emphasizes a system of interconnected people or units (i.e., network). Additionally, all five ages primarily describe the progression of faculty development in North America and the West; however, faculty development programs are burgeoning worldwide, and it seems essential to frame the emerging and future ages with recognition of the global context (Chism, Gosling, & Sorcinelli, 2008; Dezure et al., 2012; Sorcinelli & Ellozy, in press).

In the Age of the Scholar (1950s through early 1960s), the term *faculty development* referred primarily to practices for improving and advancing scholarly competence. Eble and McKeachie (1985), Rice (1996), and others noted that the key goal of professional development was to help faculty members maintain currency in their disciplines and to enhance their content expertise through sabbaticals, leaves, and fellowships to complete advanced degrees. Few colleges and universities had formal programs, and there were few measures of outcomes.

The emergence of faculty development programs during the Age of the Teacher (mid-1960s through 1970s) reflected a realization that faculty should be not only better prepared in their disciplines but also better able to teach. Thus, the goal of sustaining the vitality of faculty members as scholars expanded to emphasize the renewal and development of faculty members as teachers. Support from private foundations spurred campuses to begin to create campuswide teaching and learning centers, and by the mid-1970s, more than 40% of institutions surveyed had an individual, a program, or a set of practices that supported faculty development and teaching improvement (Centra, 1976). Faculty development also secured a professional identity in the United States through the founding of the POD Network in 1976, now the largest professional association in the world for faculty developers.

The 1980s was an important decade of growth for faculty development in the United States and abroad. During the Age of the Developer (1980s), institutions responded to critical national reports (e.g., National Commission on Excellence in Education's [1983] "A Nation at Risk") by devoting more resources toward student learning. Although faculty development kept a focus on supporting the individual instructor, interest in faculty needs at different career stages emerged during this decade as well as interest in faculty learning communities (FLCs), which emphasized collective and individual faculty growth. Programs were increasingly supported by institutional and external funds, creating heightened interest in measuring the outcomes of teaching and faculty development efforts through the evaluation of faculty members as instructors. In 1986 Erickson conducted a survey of faculty development practices, adapted from Centra's (1976) survey a decade earlier. Erickson found that at least 50% of four-year institutions offered some formal faculty development or teaching improvement services, up from about 40% a decade earlier. Significant expansion of interest in teaching development centers also occurred internationally, with such countries as Australia, Canada, and South Africa creating their own societies for teaching and learning in higher education.

The Age of the Learner (1990s) encompassed a period characterized by a changing paradigm of teaching and learning. Student learning rather than teaching took center stage; the teacher was no longer the sage on the stage pouring knowledge into empty vessels but a guide on the side facilitating student learning (Barr & Tagg, 1995). Many centers focused on assisting instructors to understand underlying theories of learning and to expand their repertoire of skills and strategies, including active learning, to adapt to the educational needs of students. At the same time, the goals and priorities of centers in the 1990s reflected new developments and complex dynamics of college teaching. There was a veritable explosion of technology use in college teaching, such as presentation tools, websites, classroom communication systems, and online courses. In addition, people at teaching and learning centers witnessed the growing attention to assessment and performance measurement, with expectations faced by individual faculty members in their classrooms as well as departments, institutions, and state systems.

Although there were no large-scale studies of the field to follow up the research of Centra (1976) and Erickson (1986), during the 1990s institutional memberships in the POD Network continued to climb as the number of teaching and learning centers increased not only in research universities but also in small colleges, comprehensive universities, and community colleges. Furthermore, the scope of center activities, including the kinds of issues faculty developers were addressing, also expanded. Demands for excellence in learning and pedagogy, and for teaching centers, expanded across the globe, triggering the creation of national-level professional societies for teaching and learning in such countries as Denmark, Finland, Germany, Ireland, New Zealand, Norway, the Netherlands, Sweden, and the United Kingdom. Interest in pedagogical issues was so strong that the International Consortium for Educational Development (ICED) was founded in 1993 with a goal of promoting development in higher education worldwide.

The findings of Sorcinelli and colleagues (2006) led us to identify the emergence of a new age for a new century, the Age of the Network. We argued that the changing nature of the student body; the professoriate; and conceptions of teaching, learning, and scholarship would increase the complexity of issues faculty developers would be asked to address. Meeting new expectations, we suggested, would require greater collaborative efforts among stakeholders such as libraries, teaching centers, instructional technology units, and assessment offices as well as academic departments and colleges. Developers expressed an interest in increasing their attention to such partnerships and to organizational change but also expressed concern about their capacity to serve faculty, administrators, institutions, and the profession simultaneously.

An Agenda for the Age of the Network

In response to the challenges posed by the Age of the Network, our original study offered a working agenda to help guide faculty development as it moved forward in the new century. We argued that one model of faculty development would not be appropriate across all institutions because contextual factors and institutional priorities matter. Taking into account that faculty development depends in part on context, we developed seven broad recommendations (along with related questions) that we believed were shared aspirations throughout the field. We urged faculty developers and institutional leaders to consider the following:

1. *Promote professional preparation and development:* The field should devote additional attention and consideration to the role of faculty development professionals, including their preparation and career paths.
2. *Inform practice with scholarship:* Faculty developers should strive to stay current with relevant research literature and ensure that research findings guide their practice.
3. *Broaden the scope of faculty development:* Faculty development should be directly aligned with institutional missions, explicitly integrated into institutional strategic plans, and supportive of the work of the faculty. Thus, institutions might organize and coordinate faculty development initiatives to address the full range of development needs faculty have in teaching and research, work-life balance, and growth across their careers.
4. *Link individual and institutional needs:* Faculty development should attend to the interests of the faculty and to larger institutional concerns. In doing so, faculty development initiatives serve as a lever for supporting faculty members' work and advancing institutional excellence, effectiveness, and quality.
5. *Context still matters:* While faculty development centers and programs share common core goals, program excellence depends on the ways a program matches its work to institutional culture; missions; and needs of students, faculty, and academic leaders.
6. *Redefine faculty diversity:* Effective faculty development programs honor and advance faculty diversity and, thus, recognize that one-size-fits-all models of faculty development should give way to programming that addresses the diversity of faculty members' needs across career stages, appointment types, gender, race, and other variables.
7. *Faculty development is everyone's work:* Effective faculty development requires institutional commitment, collaboration, and recognition that meeting individual and institutional needs is community work. In this way, faculty development communities might include not only teaching center staff but also librarians, information technologists, and professionals in assessment and student affairs.

The Higher Education Landscape Since the Age of the Network

Since the publication of *Creating the Future of Faculty Development* (Sorcinelli et al., 2006), the pace of change in a dynamic and demanding landscape of higher education has only accelerated. We argued in that volume that the Age of the Network was characterized by three dominant themes affecting faculty and their work and, thus, the field of faculty development: faculty roles; the student body; and the nature of teaching, learning, and scholarship. Indeed, the past decade has proved the accuracy of our projections concerning the importance of these three areas of continuing change.

Changing Faculty Roles

In terms of changing faculty roles, the dominant feature is the ongoing and yet dramatic shift in the nature of faculty appointments, from tenure track to non–tenure track and from full-time to part-time (Gappa, Austin, & Trice, 2007; Kezar & Sam, 2010; Schuster & Finkelstein, 2006). For example, more than two-thirds of all faculty members (full-time and part-time) currently employed in public and private higher education institutions are working in non-tenure-track contingent positions. These changes raise major questions about the nature of the faculty career, including concerns about the ways faculty members in different types of positions may commit their autonomy, time, energy, and disposition to professional development and the extent to which administrators choose to invest in the careers of those faculty. Although all faculty members should have opportunities for support through faculty development, leaders of faculty development programs and centers often face hard decisions involving where to invest time and resources as the nature of the faculty workforce shifts (Gappa et al., 2007).

Many institutions are also striving to expand the diversity of their faculty in terms of gender, race, and ethnicity. Women constitute 43% of all instructional faculty in the United States, and faculty of color are now 19% of all full-time faculty, a 30% increase in faculty of color in the past decade (Trower, 2012). However, persistent gaps remain in gender and racial parity in particular disciplines and at particular types of institutions.

At the same time, there is evidence that faculty are *aging and staying* at their institutions. Between 2000 and 2010, the proportion of all professors 65 and older nearly doubled, and the professoriate is aging at a greater rate than all other white-collar professions (Selingo, 2012). According to a survey on faculty career and retirement, among tenured faculty ages 50 and older, 49% would like and expect to work well past the retirement age of 67, another 16% would like to retire but expect to work longer, and only

35% expect to retire by age 67, suggesting that our faculties of the future will include a substantial cohort of very senior faculty (Yakoboski, 2015). How to advance and sustain the vitality of an increasingly diverse faculty in employment type as well as demographic characteristics constitutes a compelling and critically important contextual challenge facing faculty developers (Gappa et al., 2007).

Increased Focus on Student Success

Pressures relating to the success of students also constitute an important contextual ingredient relevant to faculty development today. Given the high costs of higher education, state legislatures, the federal government, and organizations such as the Gates Foundation, the Lumina Foundation, and the Institute for Higher Education Policy have been asking hard questions about access to, affordability of, and persistence through postsecondary education. At the same time, the significant personal investment by families in students' education has increased expectations for tangible student learning outcomes and faculty teaching quality. Parents and employers want to see student enrollment translate into graduation and employability.

At the national level, interest is directed toward ensuring that an increasingly diverse K–12 student body with decreasing economic resources has access to higher education and, once enrolled, moves successfully toward graduation. The College Access and Completion Agenda of the White House has called for improvements in the outcomes of higher education in terms of increased graduation rates (Olson & Riordan, 2012). At the same time, students come into higher education with a wide range of prior preparation, orientations to technology-mediated learning, and interests in how their educational experiences will relate to employment opportunities. Within this context of expectations and pressures, faculty development becomes one means for universities and colleges to support faculty members in their roles of providing effective learning experiences that result in successful student achievement and degree completion.

Changing Nature of Teaching and Learning

The changing nature of faculty work, especially in regard to teaching and learning, is closely related to the wide interest across society in student access, persistence, and success. There are strong calls for faculty members to use high-impact, evidence-based practices; for example, student-centered active learning techniques such as problem-based learning and writing across the curriculum. Funding opportunities in the science, technology, engineering, and mathematics (STEM) fields, in particular various grant programs of the National Science Foundation, have been especially important factors in encouraging systemic change processes that support the use of evidence-based teaching practices in higher education institutions. The National Academies Press's *Discipline-Based Education Research* (Singer, Nielsen, & Schweingruber, 2012) and its new book titled *Reaching Students* (Kober, 2015) are examples of high-visibility national initiatives emphasizing the need for faculty and institutional attention to reform in teaching and learning practices.

Members of various scholarly associations from across the disciplines also have devoted time in national conferences for teaching-related discussions that encourage change toward evidence-based approaches. One example of disciplinary attention to the goals and process of teaching reform is *Vision and Change in Undergraduate Biology Education* (American Association for the Advancement of Science, 2011), a report from the American Association for the Advancement of Science with support from the National Science Foundation that addresses challenges and opportunities for new approaches to teaching and learning in the field of biology. Interest in preparing future faculty for their roles as instructors has also increased considerably over the past decade. A prominent example is the Center for the Integration of Research, Teaching, and Learning (CIRTL; www.cirtl.net), which has been supported by the National Science Foundation and involves a large network of universities working together to offer professional development opportunities that help future faculty learn about the literature and research related to teaching and learning, develop their own competencies as teachers, and practice using research-based inquiry approaches to improve teaching practice and student learning.

The influence of technology on teaching and learning practices continues alongside the pressure for faculty members to use a range of evidence-based approaches. Even in universities and colleges well known for their traditional in-person residential settings, technology has become integrated into students' learning experiences. Many faculty include blended in-person and technology-mediated learning experiences and fully online courses in their teaching repertoire. Indeed, the expansion of massive open online courses (MOOCs), learning analytics, and adaptive learning systems that personalize instruction through data has made it clear that the traditional conceptions and dimensions of teaching and learning in higher education are entirely unsettled (Bass, 2012). The rise in these approaches signals a near future in which faculty and institutions will be forced to rethink the conditions of knowledge, information delivery, learning, pedagogy, and work.

Changing Landscape for Faculty Development

One implication of these trends seems to be a *ground-up* interest in strategies for and collegial interchange on teaching improvement. Faculty members are finding ways to self-organize the kind of support they feel they need. At some universities, for example, faculty members at science-oriented colleges have developed their own local faculty development programs, organized by faculty members for their colleagues. The Coalition of STEM Education Center Directors reflects this trend; it convened in a self-organized meeting in October 2014 and hosted another meeting in the summer of 2015 with support from the Association for Public and Land-grant Universities and the Alfred P. Sloan Foundation. These trends seem to have brought more attention from universities and colleges to the role of faculty development, but they also have raised questions about how to best structure faculty development opportunities and who is best situated to serve in faculty development leadership roles.

Cutting across these several developments in the past decade is continuing widespread concern about the costs of higher education. Pressures are high on universities and colleges to do more with less. One manifestation of this pressure is the heightened expectation that faculty members should be persistent and creative in seeking grant funding, not only in research universities but also in comprehensive and liberal arts colleges. In some instances, at least in research universities, faculty members are also asked to find ways to engage in entrepreneurial activities that benefit their institutions. These expectations may lead to collaborations between faculty development centers and research units to provide support to faculty members engaging in such grant-related and entrepreneurial activities. Even more relevant to all faculty developers, these pressures on faculty members mean that professional growth opportunities for faculty must be offered in time-sensitive, efficient forms that honor the multiple pressures on faculty time.

Throughout this decade of rapid change in higher education, we have observed challenges as well as exciting advancements in the field of faculty development. The percentage of formal, centralized faculty development centers continues to rise, which is documented in the following chapters. The role of teaching and learning centers as change agents has gained stronger attention. The recent and intense rise of interest in discipline- and evidence-based teaching practices, technological platforms, and learning analytics is changing the discourse on teaching and learning nationally and internationally. At the same time that we see these trends in North America, we have seen teaching and learning centers, instructional units, and new professional faculty development networks emerge in a range of countries such as China,

Croatia, Egypt, Estonia, Israel, Japan, Palestine, Saudi Arabia, Sri Lanka, Switzerland, Taiwan, and Thailand (International Consortium for Educational Development, 2014). Although this book focuses on faculty development in North America, we note colleagues working in higher education in other countries have expressed much interest in the developments discussed in this book and the models offered on this continent (Dezure et al., 2012; Sorcinelli & Ellozy, in press).

Given the dynamic context in higher education and faculty development that we have described, we judged that a follow-up examination of faculty development priorities, structures, and practices would be useful to the field. In addition, we were interested in exploring the extent to which the practices we identified as prevalent in the Age of the Network were developing or changing in response to new institutional, national, and international conditions. Thus, this current study explores anew many of the questions posed in the first study and adds others influenced by developments occurring in and outside higher education. This study resurveyed faculty developers on perceived priorities for the field as well as practices and services offered. It examined more deeply than the earlier study the organization of faculty development, including characteristics (e.g., educational background, disciplinary affiliation, experience) of directors; operating budgets and staffing levels of centers; and patterns of collaboration, reorganization, and consolidation. We also focused on what faculty developers see as their signature programs and the ways they assess the impact of their programs on teaching and learning and other key outcomes. As with our first study, we asked developers to look to the future and share their visions for the field as it approaches 2026.

The Emerging Age of Evidence

As we discuss in subsequent chapters, we see a new age already emerging: the Age of Evidence. This new age is influenced by heightened stakeholder interest in the outcomes of undergraduate education and characterized by a focus on assessing the impact of instruction on student learning, of academic programs on student success, and of faculty development within institutional mission priorities. Faculty developers are being called on to support the needs of individual faculty members and their institutions in investigating and documenting student learning. At the same time, they are being asked to address a wider range of institutional priorities and metrics of success in areas such as blended and online teaching, diversity, and the scale-up of evidence-based practices (W. G. Bowen, 2013; Schroeder & Associates, 2010; Selingo,

2013). They are being called on to broaden their audience, to address the needs of full-time, non-tenure-track faculty; part-time faculty; and graduate student instructors as well as those of pretenure and posttenure tradition-ally ranked faculty. They also are feeling increased pressure to demonstrate the return on investment of their own programs. Evidence in subsequent chapters also indicates that faculty developers are addressing the institutional needs and priorities through linkages, collaborations, and networks across institutional units. Throughout their work, faculty development profession-als are increasingly functioning as organizational change agents at the depart-ment and institutional levels, serving as experts on the needs of faculty in larger organizational discussions.

Organization of the Book

Our purpose in writing this book is to provide the field of faculty develop-ment with an important snapshot of its structures, priorities, and practices in a period of significant change and challenge in higher education. Building on and making comparisons with our prior study, we explore questions of professional preparation and pathways, programmatic priorities, collabora-tion, and assessment in multiple forms. We also look to the future of faculty development, as we did in our previous volume, using the collective wisdom of the field to identify important new directions for practice.

This introduction synthesizes the findings and recommendations from our original study (Sorcinelli et al., 2006) and highlights key forces in higher education influencing faculty development today. Chapters 1 through 7 pre-sent the results of the current study and compare those results, when pos-sible, to the findings of our prior book, offering an inventory of changes in the field from 2006 to 2016. We also focus on differences among the insti-tutional types—research universities, comprehensive universities, liberal arts colleges, and community colleges—because they continue to offer a critical contextual lens through which to view and understand faculty development practice. Chapter 1 presents a demographic portrait of the field of faculty development, including the educational backgrounds and experiences of fac-ulty developers. Chapter 2 looks at the goals guiding faculty development practice. Chapter 3 explores structures, financing, staffing, and reporting and provides profiles of the organization of faculty development at differ-ent types of institutions. Chapter 4 discusses services offered in programs, including those services developers identify as signature to their programs, and services they would expand if given the opportunity. Chapter 5 presents programming approaches being used, following a structure parallel to that of

Chapter 4. Chapter 6 looks to the future, near and far, presenting responses from developers who were asked what they believe the field should focus on in the next five years and in what directions they believe the field should and will move in the next decade. Chapter 7 discusses assessment and accountability, a key theme that emerged from the study and contributes significantly to the new age we have identified. In Chapter 8, we consider what these findings mean for the field and pose questions that can guide further reflection, discussion, and research. Each chapter concludes with highlights, which are those points we believe will be of broadest interest to readers and encapsulate the larger findings.

Conclusion

As the focus on accountability in teaching and learning, measuring student learning outcomes, and wider implementation of research-based teaching and learning practices becomes more acute, the need for research on faculty development practices increases. Further, as faculty roles continue to expand, best practices for faculty development to support faculty members across the career span and in different appointment types become more urgently needed. There is new evidence in this book that colleges and universities are assigning faculty development a more central role in leadership teams involved in institutional strategic management and change initiatives. We hope the findings presented here promote further consideration of how a networked and evidence-based approach to faculty development benefits institutions and the field.

Chapter Highlights

- This book examines the field of faculty development a decade after publication of a large-scale study of the field that explored the evolution of faculty development and offered a portrait of developers' characteristics, an analysis of faculty development services, and a summary of developers' views on priorities and future directions in the field.
- In describing the history of faculty development over a half century, the earlier study (Sorcinelli et al., 2006) described four ages: Scholar, Teacher, Developer, and Learner. It asserted that the twenty-first century brought a new age—the Age of the Network—as well as growing interest in faculty development in countries across the globe.

- External pressures on higher education institutions, and the dynamic pace of change, have had an impact on the field of faculty development over the past decade. Particularly influential trends include changes in faculty roles and the student body and the nature of teaching, learning, and scholarship. Faculty developers now work in a dynamic context that includes shifts in the patterns of faculty appointment types, strong expectations for increased access, calls for demonstrable student learning outcomes, higher graduation rates, more use of evidence-based teaching practices and instructional technologies, and continued concerns about the cost of higher education.

- Recognizing the changing context in which faculty developers work, this book presents a current portrait of faculty development professionals as well as an analysis of new directions, practices, and priorities in the field.

- We identify a new Age of Evidence for faculty development characterized by increasing focus on assessment of teaching and student learning, accreditation of academic programs, and need to demonstrate impact. Faculty developers have the opportunity and challenge to serve as a force for change within their institutions, represent faculty interests and needs, and contribute to institutional effectiveness.

WHO ARE WE?

In this chapter, we describe the design of the study. We then offer a portrait of current faculty developers, including a detailed demographic profile of faculty developers as an overall group and of faculty development directors specifically. To gain a deeper perspective on the pathways into faculty development positions, we also explore developers' educational backgrounds and immediate prior positions.

Study Design and Methodology

To update our understanding of the field, we returned to the same colleagues we studied for Sorcinelli, Austin, Eddy, and Beach (2006)—faculty and educational developers in the United States and Canada who are members of the POD Network, the largest professional association of faculty development scholars and practitioners in higher education. The original survey was mailed with postage-paid return envelopes to the 999 members of the POD Network in three waves over six weeks in 2001 and 2002. Four hundred ninety-four people returned completed surveys, yielding a 50% response rate. The survey contained 18 multipart questions regarding participant and program information, goals and purposes of faculty development programs, influences on programs and practice, current practices, and future directions. Analysis and discussion of the survey results were augmented by a review of the history of faculty development and an analysis of initiatives that won the prestigious Hesburgh Award for exceptional faculty development programs and served as examples of the services currently offered.

The new data we report here were collected in two stages. The first stage was a Web-based survey, "Creating the Future of Faculty Development: Charting Changes in the Field," which consisted of 48 questions in 10 sections. To ensure that institutional program information was provided consistently by one participant per institution, only participants who identified themselves as directors or coordinators of their programs completed the following four sections: Institutional Classification and Information, Program Structures and Finances, Program Goals and Purposes, and Collaborative Efforts. The other six sections administered to all survey participants were Faculty Developer Experience and Demographics, Audience, Program Foci, Program Approaches, Assessment of Programs, and The Future of Faculty Development. Two open-ended questions at the end of the survey asked faculty developers about their views concerning potential new directions for the field (see Appendix A).

The survey was e-mailed to the full POD Network mailing list for 2012. We also included the members of the Historically Black Colleges and Universities (HBCU) Faculty Development Network as well as the members of the Society for Teaching and Learning in Higher Education (STLHE), an organization that serves faculty developers in Canada. The survey invitations were sent in three waves to 1,382 individuals. We received completed surveys from a total of 385 individuals for an overall response rate of 28%, which was slightly higher than the 24% response rate to the latest POD Network membership survey (Winkelmes, 2011) but not quite as robust as that of our prior survey's 50% response rate.

The second stage of the current study consisted of follow-up phone interviews exploring details of participants' signature programs, which are those programs they believed were of the highest quality or were the most recognized on their campuses. As part of the survey, we asked participants to provide us with contact information on a separate form if they were willing to discuss their signature programs. Of the 385 respondents, 120 provided contact information (31%). We conducted phone interviews with participants of about 30 minutes each. The interviews followed a structured protocol that focused on the audience for the program, topic and approach used, maturity of the program, champions and challenges, and assessment of impact. We took notes throughout the interviews, rather than recording and transcribing them, so we could focus on the details of the programs. We created narrative profiles from the interview responses and asked our participants to review the narratives so the nature of the programs would be accurately portrayed.

To ensure we had a representative group of respondents, we investigated the makeup of the response set. Overall, the participants had a demographic profile almost parallel to that of the prior survey and very comparable to the most recent POD Network member survey (Winkelmes, 2011). Respondents' institutions were predominantly public and nonprofit (65%), with the exception of liberal arts colleges, which were 74% private and nonprofit. The Canadian institutions were all public. Of the institutions involved, 13% also were identified by respondents as minority-serving institutions or HBCUs.

Demographic Profile of Faculty Developers

The changing demographics of students in North American colleges and universities are well documented, as are the conversations regarding the need for the faculty and staff in these institutions to match the demographics of the student body. We were interested to see not only how diverse faculty developers are but also what their academic and professional backgrounds are and how long they have been in the field. Taken together, these characteristics can help those in the field as a whole understand its members and predict areas in need of attention to support a continually growing and thriving future.

Gender

Efforts to diversify the student bodies of higher education institutions have led to dramatic gains for women among undergraduate students and increases in the percentage of women faculty as well. Of all full- and part-time faculty in 1997, women constituted 41%. In 2013 that percentage had increased to 49% (U.S. Department of Education, 2014). Our two studies indicate gains in the number of women faculty developers as well. In our prior study, 61% of respondents were women, and 39% were men. In the current survey, as indicated in Table 1.1, 73% of respondents reported their gender as female, and 26% as male, percentages similar to those of the latest POD Network membership survey (Winkelmes, 2011). This overall pattern held across all institutional types. Comparison with data from our 2006 study also suggests that women have been entering the field at a greater rate than men over the past decade. Among the women respondents, 65% have been in the field fewer than 10 years, compared with only 55% of the male respondents. In contrast, 44% of the men have been in the field longer than 10 years, compared with only 34% of the women, which may suggest that women did not have as many opportunities to enter the field 10 or 20 years ago as they do now, or that men remain longer in faculty development. It may also reflect the reality that there were simply fewer women faculty to make a transition into faculty development.

TABLE 1.1
Gender of Respondents by Institutional Type

Gender	All	R/D	Comp	LA	CC	Can	Directors
Female	73%	73%	75%	74%	66%	66%	68%
Male	26%	26%	24%	26%	34%	34%	32%

Note. N = 329; unreported = 6. Because of rounding, some columns may not total 100%. R/D = research/doctoral institutions; Comp = comprehensive institutions; LA = liberal arts colleges; CC = community colleges; Can = Canadian institutions.

In the current survey, we were also able to look closely at the issue of gender in terms of who holds leadership positions in the field. We found that among directors, 68% were female and 32% were male. Interestingly, men hold director positions at a level somewhat higher than their proportion in the overall population of developers would suggest.

Race and Ethnicity

Through the POD Network, those in the field of faculty development have made concerted efforts to actively pursue a more diverse membership, including the establishment of a diversity committee, diversity grants, and joint meetings such as a conference in 2011 with members of the POD Network and the HBCU Faculty Development Network. The outcomes of these efforts are yet to be realized. The data suggest that Native American/American Indians, Asian/Pacific Islanders, and Black or African Americans remain but a fraction of faculty developers in the POD Network (see Table 1.2).

Among all respondents, almost 90% were White/Caucasian, a profile identical to the POD Network membership survey of 2010 (Winkelmes, 2011). Those respondents who identified themselves as Black or African American were clustered in HBCUs (12 of 16). Across primary roles and positions, we found that developers who identified themselves primarily as faculty members were more likely to identify themselves in categories other than White (see Table 1.2). However, in analyzing the race and ethnicity of faculty developers by age ranges and years in the field, we do not see an increase in diversity among newer and younger colleagues. Faculty development is a predominantly White profession, in which minorities are significantly underrepresented now and potentially into the future.

Age

In the current survey compared to the earlier one, we were able to analyze more precisely the ages of the respondents as well as their ages as related to the time they have been in their current positions. As indicated in Table 1.3, the faculty developers who responded to the survey span a wide range of ages; 23% are between 25 and 44, 31% between 45 and 54, and 41% are 55 or older. This spread across the age spectrum suggests that many developers may need to find ways to stay engaged after many years of work, while another sizable group may need mentoring to learn the ropes. Of particular note, 48% of directors are 55 or older, indicating that noteworthy leadership shifts at the institutional level and within the field are likely to occur in the next 10 to 15 years. With 72% of associate/assistant directors between ages 35 and 54, a substantial group may be functioning essentially as leaders

TABLE 1.2
Race of Respondents by Primary Role

Primary Role	American Indian or Alaska Native	Asian/ Pacific Islander	Black or African American	White/ Caucasian	Prefer Not to Answer
All positions	0%	4%	5%	89%	2%
Director	1%	3%	3%	93%	1%
Program coordinator	0%	0%	0%	100%	0%
Senior-level administrator	0%	2%	5%	88%	5%
Faculty member	0%	4%	18%	76%	2%
Associate/assistant director	0%	8%	2%	88%	2%
Technology consultant	0%	0%	0%	100%	0%
Instructional consultant	0%	7%	0.0%	90%	3%
Chairperson	0%	0%	25%	75%	0%
Educational developer	0%	33%	0%	67%	0%

Note. N = 365; unreported = 20. Because of rounding, some rows may not total 100%.

in training, presumably gaining the experience and knowledge that will enable them to be ready to step into director roles. Given the likely large number of retirements among faculty developers in the next decade, the career path into faculty development and the pathway to career advancement may need to be considered thoughtfully, with attention to expanding the diversity of the group that will be moving into senior leadership roles over the coming decade.

Institutional Type

We asked individuals to indicate the type of institution they work in because we found in our prior research that there were distinct differences in responses to many questions based on respondents' institutional type. The largest percentage of respondents (47%) comes from research or doctoral universities, a slightly greater percentage than in the earlier survey (44%; Sorcinelli et al., 2006); however, the proportion of respondents from

TABLE 1.3
Age of Respondents by Primary Role

Primary Role	25–34 Years Old	35–44 Years Old	45–54 Years Old	55–64 Years Old	65 Years and Older	Prefer Not to Answer
All	7%	21%	31%	35%	6%	1%
Director	4%	17%	31%	41%	7%	0%
Program coordinator	15%	20%	25%	30%	10%	0%
Senior-level administrator	0%	15%	39%	37%	5%	5%
Faculty member	6%	17%	31%	41%	6%	0%
Associate/ assistant director	8%	39%	33%	16%	4%	0%
Instructional consultant/ designer/ coordinator	15%	33%	21%	27%	3%	0%
Other	18%	18%	35%	24%	0%	0%

Note. N = 365; unreported = 20. Because of rounding, some rows may not total 100%.

this group accurately reflects the membership in the POD Network from research and doctoral universities, institutions that have long tended to have well-established faculty development programs. The pattern of responses from other institutional types is also comparable with the data from the earlier study (comprehensive universities, with 19% of the respondents now as compared to 23% earlier; liberal arts colleges, with 10% as compared to 11%; community colleges, with 10% of the respondents as compared to 9%; and Canadian institutions, with 9% of the respondents as compared to 8%). Table 1.4 presents the classifications of the institutions where the survey participants are located.

Primary Role

We asked participants to indicate the title they consider to be their primary title and all the other titles they hold at their institution to better understand the scope of work that faculty developers undertake (see Table 1.5). The position of director was represented most frequently across respondents, with 42% holding that title. When the roles of respondents were analyzed

TABLE 1.4
Respondents by Institutional Type

Institutional Type	All (N)	All	Directors (N)	Directors
Research/doctoral	174	47%	85	44%
Comprehensive	69	19%	43	22%
Liberal arts	38	10%	18	9%
Community college	35	10%	17	9%
Other	15	4%	8	4%
Canadian institution	32	9%	16	8%

Note. All N = 363; directors N = 187; unreported = 18.

TABLE 1.5
Primary Role by Institutional Type

Primary Role	All	R/D	Comp	LA	CC	Other	Can
Director	42%	40%	51%	35%	37%	57%	48%
Program coordinator	6%	3%	4%	5%	17%	29%	3%
Senior-level administrator	11%	10%	16%	14%	14%	14%	3%
Faculty member	15%	11%	17%	38%	14%	0%	7%
Associate/ assistant director	13%	22%	3%	8%	6%	0%	3%
Instructional consultant/other	14%	15%	9%	0%	12%	14%	36%

Note. N = 376; unreported = 9. Because of rounding, some columns may not total 100%. R/D = research/doctoral institutions; Comp = comprehensive institutions; LA = liberal arts colleges; CC = community colleges; Can = Canadian institutions.

according to institutional type, different patterns emerged. Research and doctoral institutions have a greater proportion of associate and assistant directors (22%) among developers who responded than other institutions, probably because of the need for administrative leaders to accommodate a range of responsibilities, which would be expected in large institutions. Liberal arts colleges have a greater proportion of respondents who identify primarily as faculty than is the case in other institutional types, which is not surprising in institutions where faculty are often expected to wear several different hats in their professional roles. In Canadian universities, 36% of the respondents hold positions as instructional consultants/other, a much higher proportion in that category than is the case in U.S. institutions. Differences by institutional type are further explored in following chapters.

The findings suggest that many faculty developers hold more than one position in their institution, similar to results from a decade ago. Among all respondents, 52% report two or more titles. Among directors, almost two-thirds (63%) report more than one title; 45% have faculty status as one of their other titles.

Previous Position

We were interested in the career progression of faculty developers because very little research has looked at the career paths into faculty development (McDonald, 2010). The current survey, therefore, asked participants to indicate the position they had held immediately prior to their current role. As indicated in Table 1.6, the results show that more than one-third of directors have come to their positions directly from faculty roles (35%). Another 25% were associate directors immediately prior to becoming directors. Among program coordinators and senior administrators, 33% in each category were in faculty roles immediately before assuming their current positions, and 30% of the consultant/designer/coordinators were also faculty members prior to their current roles. Twenty-eight percent of senior-level administrators reported being directors of faculty development prior to their senior-level administrator positions. Although there are some exceptions, it is clear that the most common pathway to leadership in faculty development is through

TABLE 1.6
Previous Roles of Respondents by Most Prevalent Primary Roles

	Previous Role					
Current Primary Role	*DIR*	*PC*	*SLA*	*FAC*	*AD*	*ICD*
Director	20%	9%	4%	35%	25%	6%
Program coordinator	11%	17%	6%	33%	6%	11%
Senior-level administrator	28%	5%	28%	33%	5%	0%
Faculty member	9%	6%	6%	64%	2%	4%
Associate/assistant director	9%	15%	0%	23%	17%	21%
Instructional consultant/ designer/coordinator	9%	9%	9%	30%	6%	21%

Note. Some categories in this table have been removed due to low response, resulting in cumulative percentages lower than 100%. DIR = director; PC = program coordinator; SLA = senior-level administrator; FAC = faculty; AD = associate/assistant director; ICD = instructional consultant/designer.

TABLE 1.7
Years in Faculty Development by Primary Title

Primary Type	5 Years or Fewer	6–10	11–14	15 Years or More
All	39%	31%	12%	19%
Director	33%	31%	14%	23%
Program coordinator	50%	25%	15%	10%
Senior-level administrator	20%	43%	15%	23%
Faculty member	59%	24%	2%	15%
Associate/assistant director	31%	46%	13%	10%
Other	53%	20%	10%	16%

Note. N = 371; unreported = 14. Because of rounding, some rows may not total 100%.

a faculty position. This career path pattern corresponds with the number of faculty developers who report also holding faculty status.

Years in Faculty Development

As an indicator of the degree of mobility or stability in the field, we were interested in the number of years faculty developers had held their primary positions (Table 1.7). In our 2006 study, we found a less mature directorship across the country than is reported in the current study; for example, 43% of directors reported having fewer than five years of experience in the position, a group we characterized as new developers. In the present study, that percentage has dropped to 33%. When we look at the middle years of experience, we find appreciably more directors with 6 to 10 years of experience (31% versus 24%), and with 11 to 14 years of experience (14% versus 9%), and about the same percentage of respondents who have been directors for 15 years or longer (23% versus 24%). These numbers suggest that a substantial proportion of directors has stayed in their positions, resulting in a somewhat more mature leadership group overall. Further, the fact that 23% of directors in both studies have been in their positions for 15 years or more, coupled with the previously discussed data about the age patterns among respondents, suggests that the field can anticipate significant retirements over the next decade. At the same time, however, across all respondents, 39% have been in their positions for 5 years or fewer; among directors, as noted, 33% have been in their positions for that time. Taken together, these figures indicate that those in the field should be considering ways to support the particular professional

TABLE 1.8
Highest Degree (for All Positions) Earned by Institutional Type

Highest Degree	All	R/D	Comp	LA	CC	Other	Can
Undergraduate/bachelor's degree	1%	0.6%	0%	0%	3%	0%	3%
Master's degree	23%	13%	10%	29%	51%	63%	64%
Doctoral/terminal degree	76%	86%	90%	71%	46%	37%	30%
Other	1%	0.6%	0%	0%	0%	0%	3%

Note. N = 372; unreported = 13. Because of rounding, some columns may not total 100%. R/D = research/doctoral institutions; Comp = comprehensive institutions; LA = liberal arts colleges; CC = community colleges; Can = Canadian institutions.

interests and needs of developers at different career stages. Some need opportunities and support as they gain initial experience, and others at midcareer should have professional development opportunities to prepare them to step into more senior leadership roles.

Highest Degree

To enrich our understanding of the career paths and backgrounds of faculty developers, we asked respondents to indicate their highest degree and discipline. Looking across institutional types, we found, as indicated in Table 1.8, that the work of faculty development is largely attracting individuals with substantial education; more than three-quarters (76%) of all respondents hold a doctorate or other terminal degree. At research and comprehensive universities, that percentage is closer to 90%. Only at community colleges and Canadian institutions are the percentages of master's degree holders among the developers who responded higher than that of doctorate holders. The high proportion of developers who also hold a doctoral or terminal degree aligns with the high proportion of those who hold faculty status or whose immediate prior position was in the faculty ranks, where the doctorate or comparable professional degree is expected.

Disciplinary Background

A particularly interesting demographic finding pertains to faculty developers' fields of their highest degree, presented in Table 1.9. Although we did not ask about disciplinary background in the prior study, in the current study we found that the profession of faculty development is highly eclectic in terms of drawing individuals from a wide variety of disciplines.

Although a substantial percentage of faculty developers (42%) earned their highest degree in the discipline of education (which is itself a diverse

TABLE 1.9
Respondents' Field of Highest Degree

Field	All Respondents		Faculty Respondents		Directors	
	Frequency	%	Frequency	%	Frequency	%
Education	148	42	88	28	66	36
STEM	44	13	62	20	23	12
Arts and humanities	61	17	58	18	41	22
SBE	93	27	86	27	52	28
Professional	13	4	22	7	2	1

Note. Some respondents indicated more than one field of study. STEM = science, technology, engineering, and math; SBE = social, behavioral, and economic sciences; Professional = medicine, health professions, and business.

and eclectic field), there is a solid representation among developers from the social and behavioral sciences (27%), fine arts and humanities (17%), and the STEM disciplines (13%). Also of note, developers who hold a faculty appointment come from a greater variety of disciplines, fairly equally spread among the previously mentioned areas of study. As a group, directors also receive their highest degrees across the full range of fields, although the smallest percentage (12%) hold STEM degrees. Respondents who do not hold a faculty appointment are more likely to have degrees in education.

Conclusion

The description of how the current study was conducted shows our efforts to parallel, to the greatest extent possible, key questions reported in our 2006 study while also adding questions specifically related to important issues and changes over the past decade in higher education and in the field of faculty development. The demographic, educational, and professional data presented in the chapter provide a portrait of the faculty development field and suggest issues for consideration in regard to the directions and needs of the profession in the coming years. Several critical and interconnected questions emerge when the data as a whole are reviewed: Why is the field not becoming more diverse, and what initiatives or strategies might contribute to greater diversity that reflects changes in the composition of the professoriate and the student body? What are the optimal pathways into the field and its leadership, and what factors can help shape and support such pathways? Who should take responsibility for shaping the pathways into the profession of faculty development and for the leadership of the field?

Chapter Highlights

- The field is heavily populated with women. Of the developers who responded to our current survey, 73% are women, compared with 61% of respondents reported in our 2006 study. The predominance of women is a pattern across institutional types and parallels results from a POD Network membership study (Winkelmes, 2011).
- Diversity by race or ethnicity is not characteristic of members of the profession. Almost 90% of respondents are White/Caucasian, a profile identical to that reported in the POD Network members survey (Winkelmes, 2011).
- Respondents represent a range of ages, with 41% age 55 or older and 28% between the ages of 25 and 44. Almost half of the directors are 55 or older, suggesting that substantial retirements are likely to occur in the profession in the next decade, and who is coming into the field and who is assuming leadership roles should be considered.
- The most common pathway to academic leadership for faculty developers is through a faculty position. More than half of the respondents report holding more than one institutional position, and faculty positions are most frequently mentioned as the other position.
- As a group, directors of faculty development who responded to our current survey have more years of experience in their roles than directors who responded to our prior survey. In 2006, 43% of directors reported having less than five years of experience in the position, compared with 33% in this study.
- More than three-quarters of respondents hold a doctorate or other terminal degree. Respondents' highest degrees span a wide range of fields, with 42% in education, 27% in social and behavioral sciences, 17% in fine arts and humanities, and 13% in STEM fields.

2

WHAT GUIDES OUR WORK?

This chapter presents the goals and purposes that directors report guide their programming. Our 2006 study (Sorcinelli, Austin, Eddy, & Beach, 2006) was the first study to specifically ask faculty developers which goals or purposes guided their programs. At that time, we posited that an overarching goal for faculty professional development was to improve student learning through the positive actions of individual faculty members, academic leaders, and the collective impact of faculty development programs. Hence, in our original survey, we asked respondents to indicate the degree to which their center or program was guided by 10 possible goals based on a review of the literature on faculty professional development, to add goals and purposes guiding their programs that were not listed, and to rate their influence. Based on the findings we reported in Sorcinelli and colleagues (2006), we added the following goals to the list in the current survey: (a) to help the institution respond to accreditation or quality enhancement plans and (b) to form partnerships in the learning enterprise with libraries, technology centers, research offices, and so forth. We were interested in gauging the extent to which these goals, which a decade ago were just beginning to emerge, now influenced directors' program planning.

A decade ago, we recommended that faculty development should be situated strategically within an institution's structure with active connections to and collaborations with other relevant units. Thus, the last part of this chapter discusses other campus entities that offer various kinds of faculty development and the nature of the collaborations between faculty development programs and other campus bodies.

Goals Guiding Faculty Development Programs

When analyzing the goals and purposes that guided teaching centers in our 2006 study, we first looked at responses from directors, assuming that the people in that position would have the most direct knowledge about the goals guiding faculty development in their programs. We then compared responses from the other developers who completed the survey, and found that developers at the same institution—from junior level to senior level—did not differ significantly in their choice of key goals. Given this finding, in this updated survey, we focused on responses from the senior participant in each institution. The mean results are presented in Table 2.1.

TABLE 2.1
Comparison of Goals Guiding Faculty Development Programming

Program Goals or Purposes	2006	2016
	Mean (SD)	Mean (SD)
To create or sustain a culture of teaching excellence	3.7 (.6)	3.8 (.5)
To advance new initiatives in teaching and learning	3.6 (.7)	3.7 (.5)
To respond to and support individual faculty members' goals for professional development	3.5 (.8)	3.3 (.9)
To act as a change agent within the institution	3.2 (.9)	3.3 (.8)
To provide support for faculty members who are experiencing difficulties with their teaching	3.0 (1.0)	3.1 (1.0)
To foster collegiality within and among faculty members and/or departments	3.1 (.9)	3.1 (.9)
To respond to critical needs as defined by the institution	2.9 (.9)	3.1 (.9)
To partner in the learning enterprise with libraries, technology centers, research offices, and so on	—	2.9 (.9)
To position the institution at the forefront of educational innovation	2.6 (1.0)	2.8 (1.0)
To help the institution respond to accreditation, quality enhancement plans	—	2.6 (1.0)
To support departmental goals, planning, and development	2.5 (1.0)	2.6 (.9)
To provide recognition and reward for excellence in teaching	2.5 (1.1)	2.6 (.9)
Other	—	3.6 (.8)

Note. N = 164; unreported = 29. 1 = *not at all*; 2 = *to a slight degree*; 3 = *to a moderate degree*; 4 = *to a great degree*. *Dashes indicated no data reported.*

Primary Goals

After directors had indicated the degree to which their program/unit was guided by all 12 goals, we then asked them to identify the three primary goals that influenced their programs. Across all institutional classifications, directors named the top three goals guiding their programs in the following order (percentages indicate the proportion of respondents who chose the goal as one of three primary goals for their programs, as indicated in Table 2.2):

1. Create or sustain a culture of teaching excellence: 75% (up from 72% in 2006)
2. Advance new initiatives in teaching and learning: 57% (up from 49% in 2006)
3. Respond to and support individual faculty members' goals for professional development: 29% (down from 56%)

The findings indicate that directors' ratings of the influence of particular goals, as well as the top three goals that guide faculty development programs, have remained stable over the past decade; however, the ranking and degree of emphasis for two of the top three goals has altered. Put simply, the emphasis on goals related to organizational change such as creating a culture of teaching and advancing new initiatives in teaching and learning has increased, while the importance given to responding to and supporting individual faculty members' professional development goals has decreased—quite dramatically. Also of interest is that in the top two goals, the director is the driver of change, the process is proactive, and the desired outcomes are overtly teaching oriented. In the third goal, the developer supports, facilitates, and collaborates; the process is responsive; and the desired outcomes are oriented to the broader professional goals of faculty members.

Institutional Differences

Directors of faculty development identified many of the same goals that guide their centers, but there were differences among institutional types regarding the priority of specific goals. Over the past decade, the work of directors at research and doctoral universities has coalesced around two primary goals: creating or sustaining a culture of teaching excellence (75%) and advancing new initiatives in teaching and learning (60%). All other primary goals were reported by 28% or less of research university directors.

The responses of directors in comprehensive universities look remarkably like those of respondents in research universities: focusing on creating a

TABLE 2.2

Directors' Top Three Primary Program Goals by Institutional Type

Goals	*Percentage of Directors*					
	All	*R/D*	*Comp*	*LA*	*CC*	*Can*
To create or sustain a culture of teaching excellence	75%	75%	76%	77%	71%	64%
To advance new initiatives in teaching and learning	57%	60%	58%	31%	53%	79%
To respond to and support individual faculty members' goals for professional development	29%	28%	24%	46%	41%	21%
To act as a change agent within the institution	29%	28%	29%	23%	24%	57%
To foster collegiality within and among faculty members and/or departments	19%	15%	16%	31%	35%	14%
To provide support for faculty members who are experiencing difficulties with their teaching	19%	24%	21%	15%	12%	7%
To respond to critical needs as defined by the institution	15%	18%	18%	8%	12%	7%
Other goals and purposes	13%	9%	13%	23%	12%	14%
To position the institution at the forefront of educational innovation	12%	9%	13%	23%	0%	14%
To help the institution respond to accreditation, quality enhancement plans	12%	12%	11%	8%	18%	7%
To provide recognition and reward for excellence in teaching	8%	12%	5%	0%	12%	0%
To partner in the learning enterprise with libraries, technology centers, research offices, and so on	7%	7%	8%	8%	12%	0%
To support departmental goals, planning, and development	5%	4%	3%	8%	0%	14%

Note. $N = 157$; unreported = 36. R/D = research/doctoral institutions; Comp = comprehensive institutions; LA = liberal arts colleges; CC = community colleges; Can = Canadian institutions.

culture of teaching excellence (76%) and advancing new initiatives in teaching and learning (58%). All other primary goals were reported by 24% or less of comprehensive university directors. The primary goals that guide directors at research and comprehensive institutions make sense in their university environments. Research is generally the coin of the realm, and administrators of teaching centers must find ways to advocate for good teaching in a culture in which faculty members gain more recognition and rewards from research productivity than teaching effectiveness.

Compared to their colleagues at other institutional types, liberal arts college directors reported a wider range of priorities. Beyond creating a culture of excellence (77%), they were more likely to rank "respond to and support individual faculty members' goals for professional development" (46%) and "foster collegiality within and among faculty members and/or departments" (31%) among their top goals and less likely to choose "advance new initiatives in teaching and learning" (31%). These findings may reflect the centrality of the traditional emphasis on teaching at small colleges, the recognition of the need for a teaching-committed and responsive faculty, and the emphasis on academic community as a core cultural value of liberal arts colleges. Of note is a robust focus on support for individual faculty members and for developing collegiality and interdisciplinary interactions.

Interestingly, community college directors reported that their centers were guided by goals that in part mirrored those of the research and comprehensive universities, and in part those of small liberal arts colleges. Faculty development in community colleges is increasingly called on to respond to external pressures and address institutional initiatives. Their top four guiding goals were creating and sustaining a culture of teaching excellence (71%), advancing new initiatives in teaching and learning (53%), responding to and supporting individual faculty members' goals for professional development (41%), and fostering collegiality within and among faculty members and/or departments (35%). These findings suggest that community college faculty development seeks to balance goals tied to institutional mission and external needs as well as those supporting faculty and collegial priorities.

The top three goals that guide faculty development programs among Canadian directors show some major changes in degree of emphasis from the previous decade. All three of their top goals are overtly organizational-change oriented or teaching oriented. To advance new initiatives in teaching and learning moved to the primary position, from 40% in 2006 to 79% in 2016. Acting as a change agent within the institution moved from 20% in 2006 to 57% in 2016. Creating a culture of teaching excellence decreased slightly, from 74% in 2006 to 64% in 2016. Much like with their U.S. counterparts, responding to and supporting individual faculty members' goals for professional development declined dramatically, from 56% in 2006 to 21% in 2016.

These findings may reflect a response to the emergence of the research university model in Canada, which has increased significantly over the past decade. The change has brought enhanced prestige to universities and more funding options. However, there is a sense that the rise in research intensity has brought demanding (and perhaps detrimental) challenges to undergraduate education and added stress to faculty. In response, there has been an increasing emphasis, particularly in the research-intensive universities, on addressing the balance between teaching and research (Bradshaw, 2013). Our findings suggest that Canadian developers are proactively addressing the growing pressure to improve teaching quality.

Least Influential Goals

The goals least chosen by directors are as interesting as those most chosen. Goals that the fewest number of respondents chose as primary among their top three guiding forces included the following (again, these overall percentages refer to the proportion of directors who chose the item among their top goals):

- help the institution respond to accreditation, quality enhancement plans (12%, new question);
- provide recognition and reward for excellence in teaching (8%, down from 13% in 2006);
- form partnerships in the learning enterprise with libraries, technology centers, research offices, and so on (7%, new question); and
- support departmental goals, planning, and development (5%, roughly equal to 7% in 2006).

According to directors, the least influential goal is to support departmental goals, planning, and development, which is nearly identical to the rankings of directors in our 2006 study. At that time, we suggested that the finding may have reflected the field's traditional focus on either individual faculty or campuswide programs rather than on targeted or customized support to departments. We also suspected that it may have indicated developers' awareness of the limited resources to broadly support the needs and goals of all departments. We now have increasing evidence in the larger higher education literature, however, that supporting department-focused implementation of faculty development, course and curriculum development, and assessment of student learning is critical to widespread and lasting change in faculty teaching practices and the reward structures that recognize such efforts (Fry, 2014). This goal may become more influential in the next decade as centers develop and share models and practices for working directly with departments to effect faculty, instructional, and curricular change.

Directors reported that forming partnerships in the learning enterprise with other related units was also a less influential goal for centers. Over the past decade, a number of other units have become engaged in faculty development (e.g., individual schools and colleges within universities, offices of assessment, academic computing, libraries, and STEM teaching and learning centers). Likewise, networking with other units is a key strategy to increase the reach of faculty development. Therefore, the weak showing of this goal surprised us. It does, however, align with the responses reported regarding collaborations with other units, discussed in the next section. It may be that current structures of university support units, different cultures among those units, and limited staffing and resources simply don't allow for the kinds of partnerships that would more holistically support faculty. In particular, directors may find that time limitations make collaborative relationships difficult to develop and maintain.

Another less influential goal is that of providing recognition and reward for excellence in teaching. In fact, this goal is something that many centers put into practice through teaching awards, grants, and fellowships. Administering the college's or university's major teaching awards and grants is a common charge of centers and often more closely associates them with commitment to and focus on outstanding teaching (Cook & Kaplan, 2011). At the same time, directors may see this as a less influential goal, because providing rewards for teaching is related to the recognition of teaching effectiveness in personnel decisions such as tenure, promotion, and merit. These rewards are primarily located at the department level and are further related to an institution's valuation of teaching. If such values are not embedded in institutional culture—from departments to the provost's office—it is difficult for the teaching center to provide meaningful recognition of rewards for teaching.

Over the past decade, regional accrediting associations have modified their criteria to inculde evidence of student learning and the professional development of faculty as instructors. Although our findings indicate that a small percentage of centers is guided by the primary goal of helping their institution respond to accreditation and quality enhancement plans, it is not currently driving the agenda of most programs. Developers do, however, see this as a future direction for the field (discussed in Chapters 6 and 7). As we argue in later chapters, this goal may become more influential in the next decade.

Already, some regional accreditors have turned their attention to encouraging continual improvement through quality enhancement plans and projects, which some faculty development programs have taken the lead on and which more programs may adopt in the future (Sorcinelli & Garner, 2013).

Collaborations

One of the hallmarks of a networked faculty development enterprise is collaboration across campus to reach a range of audiences, increase the visibility of faculty development opportunities, and maximize available resources. Furthermore, recent reports across the United States about institutional projects to reform teaching and learning processes invite questions about the extent to which developers work with other academic and support units. We asked directors to rate the extent to which other units offer faculty development programming on their own and the extent to which directors collaborate with those units. Table 2.3 reports the percentage of respondents who answered that they collaborated with particular units *to a moderate extent* or *to a great extent* and who indicated that other units offer faculty development services independently *to a moderate extent* or *to a great extent*.

The data indicate that faculty developers do collaborate at least to some extent with several other units, although such collaborations do not appear to be extensive. Where collaborations are happening, they are on a moderate scale. Technology centers are the most common partners by far (3.2 on a 4-point scale); 77% of respondents indicate they collaborate with these units to a *moderate* or *great extent*. Academic deans are also fairly frequent partners (2.9); 64% of directors indicate that they work together to a *moderate* or *great extent*. A majority of directors indicate significant collaboration with libraries (2.7) and assessment offices (2.5). Community/service-learning offices, writing centers, offices of diversity and inclusion, and teaching assistant (TA) support and development programs constitute a second tier of collaboration with means between 2.2 and 2.4; 40% to 49% of respondents indicate moderate to great engagement with them. Interestingly, responses do not vary in meaningful ways across institutional types, and we therefore chose to report the data only in aggregate form. A small number of directors indicated that some of the functions (in particular, technology training or TA development) were housed in their centers already. Several indicated that their institutions do not have units addressing the areas listed, in particular, assessment offices. Of the entities named when a respondent indicated collaborating with a unit other than those offered, disability services for students came up most frequently, followed by distance and e-learning offices.

TABLE 2.3

Collaboration With and Services Offered by Other Campus Units

Campus Unit	Rate of Collaboration With Other Units			Rate of Other Units Offering Programming		
	N Responding	Mean	% 3 or 4	N Responding	Mean	% 3 or 4
Technology centers	151	3.2	77	147	3.0	67
Deans/assistant/ associate deans (in colleges)	150	2.9	64	144	2.3	41
Libraries	141	2.7	59	152	2.3	36
Assessment offices	136	2.5	54	133	1.8	17
Community/ service-learning	132	2.4	49	135	2.2	37
Writing centers	139	2.3	42	135	2.1	30
Offices of diversity/inclusion	139	2.3	42	132	1.9	18
TA support and development	119	2.2	40	122	1.9	27
Graduate college	121	2.1	37	123	1.5	11
Research affairs	131	2.1	34	137	2.0	28
Student affairs and residence life	129	2.0	26	120	1.6	9
International affairs/study abroad	128	1.9	25	122	1.6	11
Federal, state, or foundation grants	119	1.8	23	108	1.7	13
Campus sustainability offices	116	1.6	16	103	1.4	5
Honors college	120	1.5	13	111	1.3	5

Note. 1 = *not at all*; 2 = *to a slight extent*; 3 = *to a moderate extent*; 4 = *to a great extent*. Percentage represents proportion of respondents for each question who chose *moderate extent* or *great extent* regarding collaboration and services offered by other units.

Directors reported that some other campus units are also offering faculty development programming but generally not extensively. Those most frequently offered faculty development include technology centers (mean = 3.0, 67% *moderate* or *great extent*), offices of academic deans such as a dean of faculty or college dean (mean = 2.3, 41% *moderate* or *great extent*), and libraries (mean = 2.3, 36% *moderate* or *great extent*). About a third of directors indicated that the community/service-learning offices and writing centers at their institutions were offering development to faculty. Generally, however, faculty developers did not perceive much relevant programming emerging from other units on campus.

Conclusion

The shifts in the focus and magnitude of primary goals reported by directors can, to a certain extent, be seen as parallel to the changes in center structures toward centralization, which is discussed in Chapter 3. The current primary goals address institutional change and place the director as a change agent to a much greater extent than those we reported in 2006. The historic focus on the needs of individual faculty members is still among the top goals guiding centers, but to a lesser extent than a decade ago. Three of the goals currently reported as least influential—supporting departmental goals and development, helping the institution respond to accreditation, and working with other units on campus—are identified by developers in later chapters as areas to address in the future.

Collaborations with other units on campus were less extensive than we expected. Although more than 75% of responding directors indicated moderate to extensive collaboration with technology centers, in general, significant collaboration was not the norm, and other units on campus beyond technology centers were not offering programs to faculty.

Chapter Highlights

- The three primary goals that guide faculty development programs have remained constant over the past decade; however, the rankings for two of the top three goals have changed. The emphasis on creating or sustaining a culture of teaching, and advancing new initiatives in teaching and learning has increased, while the importance given to responding to and supporting individual faculty members' professional development goals has decreased significantly.

- Directors in different types of institutions identified many of the same goals as guiding their programs, but the priority of specific goals differed. Research and doctoral university directors identified two primary goals: creating or sustaining a culture of teaching excellence and advancing new initiatives in teaching and learning. Liberal arts colleges and community colleges were guided by a wider range of goals, including more emphasis on individual and collegial support.
- Goals that the fewest number of respondents chose as primary guiding forces have not shifted measurably over the past decade. Of least importance are supporting departmental goals, planning and development, forming partnerships in the learning enterprise with other units, and providing recognition and reward for excellence in teaching.
- It is worth noting that goals currently identified as least influential are reported in other areas of the data as key to advancing a culture of teaching and learning going forward.
- Collaborations with technology centers are strong, and those with deans or associate deans of colleges, libraries, and assessment offices are somewhat prevalent but moderate.

3

WHERE AND WITH WHOM
DO WE WORK?

W hile goals and purposes guide the work of programs, the structure that organizes faculty development in an institution is an important factor in determining the character of a center. This chapter discusses the ways faculty development is organized, funded, and situated in relation to other units in an institution. It discusses the structures that institutions use to address faculty development and compares the prevalence of different types of structures to those reported in Sorcinelli, Austin, Eddy, and Beach (2006). More than in the past, faculty development seems to be recognized as important to institution-wide priorities. This chapter also considers patterns in budgets and staffing for faculty development centers, which indicate some of the investments institutions are making to support teaching, learning, and faculty work.

Structures

To better understand how faculty development efforts are currently structured in institutions, and how those structures have changed over the decade, we asked developers what best described the structure of faculty development efforts at their institutions: a single centralized unit with dedicated staff, a clearinghouse for programs and offerings sponsored across the institution but offering few programs itself, a committee charged with supporting faculty development, an individual faculty member or administrator charged with supporting faculty development, or structures such as a systemwide office. The descriptions are parallel to the options in the previous study as well as from earlier research and literature on faculty development (Centra, 1976; Erickson, 1986; Wright, 2002). To avoid multiple responses from the same institution, the current survey asked for data on structures only from directors or senior administrators with faculty development oversight.

A decade ago, the findings showed an increase in the proportion of centralized units with dedicated staff in comparison to patterns reported in earlier research (Erickson, 1986). This trend toward more formalization and centralization has continued, as illustrated in the latest findings that show that the organizational structure for faculty development programs is most often coordinated by an identifiable, centralized unit with professional staff (59% in this study compared to 54% in the prior study). The next most frequent structure involves an individual faculty member or administrator tasked with overarching responsibilities for faculty development. This structure is used by almost one third (29%) of the institutions today, an increase from 19% a decade ago. Structures centered on committees planning faculty development, or clearinghouses of institutional resources have declined. In 2006, 16% of respondents reported having one of those structures. Only 3% of the respondents indicated such a structure now. Table 3.1 summarizes the data from the current survey concerning the organizational structure of programs.

Institutional Differences

Although the overall trend across campuses is toward more formalized and centralized faculty development programs, some variation in structures is evident across institutional types. Research and doctoral universities overwhelmingly organize their faculty development programs as campus-wide centers

TABLE 3.1
Faculty Development Structure by Institutional Type

Title	All	R/D	Comp	LA	CC	Can
Clearinghouse	1%	0%	3%	0%	0%	1%
Committee	3%	3%	0%	8%	12%	3%
Individual	29%	19%	33%	62%	47%	32%
Central unit	59%	70%	59%	31%	41%	58%
Structures such as a system-wide office	2%	1%	3%	0%	0%	2%
Special-focus unit that supports FD but is not a comprehensive FD office	1%	6%	3%	0%	0%	1%
Other	4%	1%	0%	0%	0%	3%

Note. N = 165; unreported = 28. Because of rounding, some columns may not total 100%. FD = faculty development; R/D = research/doctoral institutions; Comp = comprehensive institutions; LA = liberal arts colleges; CC = community colleges; Can = Canadian Institutions.

that serve the entire institution or a substantial segment of it. The percentage reporting such a structure has not changed much across a decade. Data reported in our 2006 study showed that 72% of these institutions identified that structure, compared to 70% in this study. At the same time, at research and doctoral institutions, the model of an experienced faculty member or academic leader who directs faculty development efforts increased from 10% a decade ago to 19% today.

Responses from comprehensive universities indicated an increased presence of centralized units (59%, up from 51%). Also, and similar to research and doctoral universities, the model of an individual responsible for faculty development remains a viable and, in fact, an increasingly prevalent structure at a number of comprehensive universities (33%, up from 24%).

Centra (1976) found that many small liberal arts colleges, in comparison to larger institutions, were much less able or inclined to support a formalized structure for faculty development. However, at the time of our earlier study, more than half the liberal arts colleges participating had either a faculty member or an administrator in charge of faculty development (33%) or a formal unit (26%). From the last study to the current one, formalization has nearly doubled, either through movement to an individual in charge of initiatives (62%) or to a centralized center (31%). In contrast, the use of committees to support faculty development has declined precipitously. In our 2006 study, one-quarter (26%) of the liberal arts colleges reported the use of committees to coordinate faculty development, but the current data show that only 8% identified a committee as the structure at their college. Among institutional types, small liberal arts colleges have demonstrated the most significant movement toward formalized structures for faculty development in the past decade.

Faculty development structures in community colleges have also moved dramatically toward centralization. A decade ago, community colleges showed the most variation in structure with more than a third reporting central units (35%), while the other two-thirds organized their faculty development through either individual leaders (21%), committees (21%), or clearinghouses (17%). In this study, the only models reported were an individual responsible for faculty development (47%), a centralized unit (41%), and a committee structure (12%). Clearinghouses were not mentioned. Clearly, faculty development has become more centralized and integrated into strategy considerations for these colleges.

Canadian universities also showed changes in their structures over the past decade, although the patterns are somewhat different from those of their U.S. counterparts. Canadian institutions still have a strong preference for centralized units with dedicated staff (58%); however, in the earlier study, that

TABLE 3.2
Length of Time in Current Faculty Development Structure

Title	N	<5 Years	6–10 Years	11–20 Years	>21 Years
Total	159	33%	23%	34%	9%
Central unit	99	24%	24%	37%	15%
Individual	48	45%	23%	31%	0%
Clearinghouse	2	50%	0%	50%	0%
Committee	5	60%	20%	20%	0%

Note. N = 159; unreported = 34. Because of rounding, some rows may not total 100%.

percentage was 71%. The latest data show that although the percentage with centralized units has dropped, a greater proportion of institutions now rely on individual faculty members or administrators who are responsible for faculty development (an increase for this model from 16% in the previous results to 32% in the current study).

Years in Current Structure

There is further evidence in the data of noteworthy shifts in the organization of faculty development on campuses. In this study, directors were asked a new follow-up question about the structure reported in Table 3.1, to further understand how long faculty development offices or programs existed in their current structures (Table 3.2). More than half of respondents (56%) reported their current structures are 10 or fewer years old, and fully a third (33%) have structures that are 5 or fewer years old. Interestingly, only 9% of respondents have had their current structure 21 or more years, reflecting research that finds centers are continually subjected to reorganization, creating new opportunities and stresses on structures and staff (Chism, Gosling, & Sorcinelli, 2010). Having said that, the overall growth over the past 5 to 10 years in centralized structures suggests that faculty development is seen as increasingly important to the mission of institutions. Whether faculty development is yet seen as a strategic imperative in the context of increasing demands on faculty members and their institutions is not completely clear. However, in terms of structures, institutions clearly are moving faculty development from the margins toward the core of the institution.

Reporting Lines and Staffing, Budgets, and Resources

The current survey asked directors several new questions about their reporting lines, staffing levels, budgets, and supplementary resources. We were interested in creating a comprehensive profile of faculty development that could be useful for directors and senior administrators in calibrating the scope and size of their efforts.

Direct Reporting

Early in the development of the field, teaching centers were situated in a variety of locations in higher education institutions, including academic affairs offices, schools of education, libraries, and audiovisual centers. As the field has matured, we see a formalization of reporting lines and more direct and prominent placement of centers and programs within the domains of chief academic officers—the provost, associate provost, or the dean of faculty. These reporting shifts align with the movement toward centralization of faculty development structures. Table 3.3 provides details regarding reporting lines at different types of institutions. Across institutional types, many directors of faculty development report to either the provost of the institution (33%) or the associate, assistant, or vice provost (45%). This pattern is particularly pronounced in research and doctoral universities and comprehensive institutions. In liberal arts colleges and community colleges, a greater proportion report to deans and associate, assistant, or vice provosts rather than to provosts. It is worth noting, however, that the supervising dean might very well be the dean of faculty or of the college, a role parallel to that of the provost in a research university. The somewhat more varied reporting lines in liberal arts and community colleges may also reflect the

TABLE 3.3
Reporting Structure: To Whom Do Directors Report?

Directors Reports to	All	R/D	Comp	LA	CC	Can
N	161	71	39	13	16	14
President	1%	0%	0%	0%	6%	0%
Provost	33%	32%	46%	46%	19%	14%
Associate/assistant/ vice provost	45%	54%	46%	15%	25%	36%
Dean/associate dean	13%	9%	5%	31%	25%	29%
Vice president/ vice chancellor	6%	6%	0%	0%	25%	14%
Other	3%	0%	3%	8%	0%	7%

Note. N = 161; unreported = 32. Because of rounding, some columns may not total 100%. R/D = research/doctoral institutions; Comp = comprehensive institutions; LA = liberal arts colleges; CC = community colleges; Can = Canadian institutions.

flatter organizational structures of these institutions compared to those of larger universities.

Staffing

The average number of staff who work in faculty development at different institutional types is reported in Table 3.4. We asked directors to indicate the number of full-time equivalent (FTE) positions they had in their centers, assuming that some positions might be part-time. The range of responses was very high; the standard deviations for some positions were far larger than the means. A few directors reported very extensive staffs; those of centralized units typically indicated they had one full-time director (only 20 of 155 respondents indicated that as director they were less than full-time), one to two associate or assistant directors, a handful of professional staff, and a mix of support staff, graduate students, and undergraduate students. Comprehensive universities and community colleges are more likely to have directors appointed less than full-time and to have relatively lean staffs.

Budget for Programming

We asked directors to report the size of their programming budgets excluding staff salaries. The rationale for this approach was that the staffing information shows institutional investment in personnel for faculty development, but the additional budget information reflects investment beyond staff, such as in grants for faculty, funds for event planing and facilitation, initiatives for participation, and traval. The majority (70%) of respondents reported that they operate on annual programming budgets under $100,000. Large research/doctoral universities were most likely to have more robust budgets for programming. This is not a surprising situation, given their size and the range of constituencies they often serve (e.g., graduate students, full- and part-time faculty, academic leaders). Almost half the directors indicated they were offering programming on annual budgets under $50,000, this being especially true of comprehensive universities (65%), community colleges (59%), and liberal arts colleges (54%). Table 3.5 reports the percentages of programs at different types of institutions that operate in particular budget ranges.

Additional Funding

Programming budgets do not tell the full story of faculty development funding. Seeking information on the full scope of revenue that programs use, we asked directors to indicate (*yes* or *no*) whether they received funds from

TABLE 3.4

Average Number of Staff by Institutional Classification

Title	All Mean (SD)	RD Mean (SD)	Comp Mean (SD)	LA Mean (SD)	CC Mean (SD)	Can Mean (SD)
Director	1.01 (.42)	1.07 (.47)	.96 (.33)	1.02 (.35)	.69 (.38)	.88 (.26)
Assistant/associate director	1.72 (2.76)	2.38 (3.44)	.61 (.59)	1.00 (1.22)	.33 (.58)	1.33 (.98)
Academic/professional/ consulting staff	3.58 (4.04)	3.36 (3.30)	2.49 (2.90)	4.24 (6.08)	1.56 (2.50)	5.36 (4.18)
Support or secretarial staff	1.84 (3.02)	2.48 (3.99)	.83 (.56)	1.31 (1.05)	.77 (.40)	2.73 (3.13)
Graduate students	2.83 (5.89)	3.76 (7.11)	.84 (.94)	.00 (.00)	—	5.00 (3.56)
Undergraduate students	3.52 (10.38)	5.23 (13.40)	1.40 (1.51)	.94 (1.42)	—	1.60 (.55)
Other	8.30 (27.87)	.67 (1.21)	1.00 (1.41)	—	.83 (.14)	55.00 (70.71)

Note. N = 161; unreported = 32; RD = research/doctoral institutions; LA = liberal arts colleges; CC = community colleges; Can = Canadian institutions. Dashes indicate no data reported.

TABLE 3.5
Program Budget by Institutional Type

Budget	All	R/D	Comp	LA	CC	Can
N	147	60	37	13	17	12
$0–$24,999	30%	18%	41%	31%	35%	31%
$25,000–$49,999	18%	13%	24%	23%	24%	15%
$50,000–$99,999	22%	22%	24%	38%	12%	15%
$100,000–$149,999	10%	13%	5%	8%	6%	8%
$150,000–$199,999	7%	7%	3%	0%	12%	23%
$200,000–$249,999	5%	10%	3%	0%	0%	0%
>$250,000	8%	17%	0%	0%	12%	8%

Note. N = 148; unreported = 45. Because of rounding, some columns may not total 100%. R/D = research/doctoral institutions; Comp = comprehensive institutions; LA = liberal arts colleges; CC = community colleges; Can = Canadian institutions.

TABLE 3.6
Additional Funding Sources by Institutional Type

Funding Sources	All	R/D	Comp	LA	CC	Can
N	160	71	37	12	16	15
External grants	32%	29%	33%	39%	29%	47%
Endowment/gift funds	24%	28%	19%	22%	18%	24%
Carryover funds	20%	32%	5%	6%	12%	24%
Onetime university allocations for special projects	41%	42%	42%	33%	41%	47%
Cost share with other units	30%	33%	33%	22%	24%	29%
Fees for service (programs/events/ conferences) internal and external	5%	6%	7%	0%	0%	6%
Union money/contract negotiations (buyouts, negotiated funds, etc.)	2%	2%	0%	6%	0%	0%
Fund-raising	1%	0%	5%	0%	0%	0%
None	17%	18%	26%	0%	18%	0%

Note. N = 160; unreported = 33. R/D = research/doctoral institutions; Comp = comprehensive institutions; LA = liberal arts coleges; CC = community colleges; Can = Canadian institutions. Mean number of funding sources reported was 2.33.

a variety of sources in the prior two years. Table 3.6 presents, by institution type, the percentage funds garnered by directors beyond annual budgets from particular sources. The average number of sources directors reported accessing was 2.33.

The data suggest that faculty developers at every institutional type are actively entrepreneurial. As a group, fewer than 20% of the reporting institutions have received no additional funds beyond their base program budget in the past two years, although it is noteworthy that about one quarter (26%) of the comprehensive institutions indicated receiving no additional funding. Generally, directors reported using a patchwork of support to respond to faculty and institutional needs. For example, 41% of directors reported that their programs receive onetime allocations for taking on special institutional projects, 32% reported that their programs bring in external grant funding, 30% reported cost-share initiatives with other units, and 24% received some revenue from endowment or gift funds. Very few programs charge fees for services, suggesting that centers strive to be service oriented, and a fee-for-service process has not been a widely used mechanism to balance or enhance budgets. Even fewer programs are actively fund-raising.

Portraits of Structural Features Across Institutional Types

When the responses regarding structures, funding, and staffing are considered by institutional type, distinctive overall portraits emerge. In the following sections, data previously presented in this chapter are used to create structural portraits of faculty development programs.

Research and Doctoral Universities

Research and doctoral institutions are most likely to have centralized units (70%) with dedicated staffing. Only 20% of directors report having fewer than two individuals charged with faculty development. These structures are fairly mature; 59% of them have been in place 6 to 20 years, and only 19% report their structure to be less than 5 years old. Directors most often report to an associate or vice provost (54%) or directly to the provost (32%; Table 3.3). Centers in research and doctoral institutions have a broad range of programming budgets, but 60% are under $200,000 per year. More than 40% of directors report annual budgets of under $100,000. These budgets are augmented by a wide variety of funds. Directors report having access to onetime funds for special projects (42%), cost-sharing with other units (33%), using carry-over funds from prior fiscal years (32%), securing external grants (29%), and tapping into endowment funds (28%). Among these directors, only 18% reported having no other funds aside from their base program-ming budgets. Looking at the staff configuration at research and doctoral universities, a full-time director, one or two associate or assistant directors, and a small mix of instructional design staff and administrative staff appear to be most common. The median number of FTE positions across all roles reported is 8; the mode or most often reported number is 1. In other words, although several centers report a larger number of staff, many have only a single FTE in each position category.

Comprehensive Universities

Comprehensive universities are most likely to have a centralized unit with dedicated staff (60%) or an individual charged with the oversight of faculty development (33%). Directors reported that these structures have been in place for a lesser period of time than those at research and doctoral uni-versities. In regard to current structures, 46% of units in comprehensive universities are strikingly new, with 15% in place fewer than 3 years and 31% between 3 and 5 years. That said, 31% of the directors reported that their current structure had been in place 11–20 years. Directors report to the provost (46%) or to an associate or vice provost (46%). Budgets reported are typically under $100,000. Of note, 48% of directors reported budgets between $25,000 and $99,000, and another 41% indicated their budgets are under $25,000. Other funds that directors have access to include onetime funding for special projects (42%), cost sharing with other units (33%), and external grants (33%). Directors did not report much use of carry-over or endowment funds, and 26% reported no additional funding sources beyond their base budgets. Programs have a median of three FTE staff, and a mode of two, indicating that staffs in comprehensive universities are fairly uniform in size.

Liberal Arts Colleges

Liberal arts college directors are more likely to be the single individual charged with faculty development as part of their duties (61%) and less likely to head a centralized unit (31%). A substantial majority (62%) of directors reported that their current structure has been in place 5 years or fewer. A subgroup of directors (15%) reported 6 to 10 years in their current structure, and another 15% reported 11 to 20 years. Directors report to the provost (46%), a dean or associate dean (31%), or an associate or vice provost (15%). Almost all directors (92%) reported annual budgets under $100,000; 31% reported budgets less than $25,000. Those relatively small base budgets are augmented, however, by external grants (39%, the highest percentage across institutional types), onetime funds for special projects (33%), cost sharing with other units (22%), and endowment or gift funds (22%). All directors reported some kind of augmentation of their base funding. Across all categories of staff roles, the median number reported was two, and the mode was one; the faculty development staffs at liberal arts colleges are uniformly lean.

Community Colleges

Community college directors reported a greater percentage of centralized units (41%) than did liberal arts directors, but the majority report that a single individual is responsible for faculty development (47%). The structures in community colleges seem fairly stable; 64% of the directors reported 11 to 20 years in their current structure. Reporting lines are varied—in fact, the most varied among all institutional types. Directors report to vice presidents or vice-chancellors (25%), vice or associate provosts (25%), deans or associate deans (25%), or the provost (19%). Faculty development at community colleges operates on a wide range of budgets. Thirty-five percent of directors indicated that their operating budgets are below $25,000 per year. However, a small percentage (12%) indicated budgets of over $250,000, which we note is quite unusual and likely reported by centers that serve a community college system. A large percentage (41%) indicated that they receive onetime funding for special projects, 29% report external grants, and 24% report cost sharing with other units on campus. Eighteen percent of directors indicated that they have no other funds beyond their annual program budgets. Staffs are generally small. The median and mode of all roles are one FTE.

Canadian Institutions

Directors of Canadian institutions reported centralized units as their most prevalent structure (58%), followed by individuals charged with faculty development (32%). The majority have had that structure for 11 to 20 years (64%). Directors in these institutions report to a variety of supervisors: 36% report to associate or vice provosts, 29% to deans or associate deans, 14% to provosts, and 14% to vice presidents or vice-chancellors. Budgets are also varied. Thirty-one percent of directors reported annual budgets of less than $25,000 and another 30% indicated that their programs receive between $25,000 and $100,000, but 23% reported budgets between $150,000 and $199,000. Canadian directors reported considerable access to additional funds compared to directors at U.S. institutions. They augment their budgets through external grants (47%), onetime funds (47%), cost sharing with other units (29%), and endowment and carryover funds (both 24%). All reported at least one other source of funding that supplements their annual program budget. The median number of staff in Canadian centers is five—a full-time director, a half- or full-time associate or assistant director, three or four professional or consulting staff, and an administrative support position.

Conclusion

The past decade has seen a continued consolidation and centralization of faculty development structures toward centers with dedicated staff and designated individuals (often identified as directors). The movement is most dramatic at liberal art colleges and community colleges, both of which experienced a doubling of the number of individuals charged with faculty development and strong increases in centralized units, and a corresponding drop in other kinds of structures. For most institutions, the investment in personnel seems to be the largest share of resources allocated for faculty development; annual programming budgets separated from personnel costs are modest across institutional types. Perhaps because of this budget situation, faculty development directors are highly entrepreneurial; more than 80% reported obtaining funds from a variety of other sources to augment their annual program budgets.

Chapter Highlights

- The organizational structure for faculty development programs has become more formalized and centralized in the past decade (as reported in this study as compared to 2006). It is most often coordinated by an identifiable, centralized unit with professional staff (59%, up from 54% in 2006). In addition, a structure in which a faculty member or administrator has overarching responsibility for faculty development has increased at all institutional types (29%, up from 19% in 2006).
- The pattern in reporting lines also supports the conclusion that the structure of faculty development is becoming more centralized. Seventy-eight percent of directors report to either their provost or an associate or vice provost (Table 3.3). This shift toward greater centralization is relatively new. That is, more than half of respondents (56%) reported that their current structures are 10 or fewer years old, and fully a third reported structures that are five or fewer years old (see Table 3.2).
- Few directors reported extensive staffs. Centralized units typically have one full-time director; one to two associate or assistant directors;

a handful of professional staff; and a mix of support staff, graduate students, and undergraduate students. Median staffing numbers range from one to eight depending on institutional type.

- The majority (70%) of directors reported that they operate on annual programming budgets under $100,000. Forty-eight percent report annual budgets under $50,000 (Table 3.5).

- Institutional differences in center structure, budget, and staffing create distinct profiles of faculty development support at different types of institutions.

4

SERVICES WE FOCUS ON

The work of centers for teaching and learning has evolved since their beginnings in the late 1960s, propelled by changes in the professoriate; the student body; and the nature of teaching, learning, and scholarship (Sorcinelli, Austin, Eddy, and Beach 2006). In this chapter, we present the issues and areas currently being addressed by centers through their services and programming. We first look at the most prominent issues undergirding current services offered by centers and, whenever possible, compare the results with the findings of our 2006 study, to highlight continuity and change over the last decade.

In the present study, we decided to explore more deeply the programs that are most valued by developers, that is, their signature services. These are the services that centers are recognized for, that garner the greatest participation, that address key needs developers see in their institutions. We therefore asked participants to choose up to three services they considered their center's signature offerings. Respondents also provided contact information on a separate online form if they were willing to participate in a follow-up telephone interview that would allow us to gather details about their signature programs. Some 120 individuals provided contact information, 70 of whom were available and were interviewed. Short profiles of several selected programs are presented in this chapter to illuminate survey results and to exemplify the range of signature services. Finally, we explored the services developers are less likely to address in their programs as well as the services they would most like to add to their portfolios if they were given the opportunity or additional resources to do so.

Current Faculty Development Services

Our 2006 study was the first to ask faculty developers about the major issues their centers address through the array of services they offer. In this survey, we again asked developers the extent to which their programs are currently offering services pertaining to selected issues. Participants responded to a list of 39 issues, divided into three key areas: teaching and learning (14 issues), faculty work and career development (16 issues), and educational or institutional improvement (9 issues). The list contained the majority of items from the prior survey (a few that had garnered almost no response were removed) as well as a selected few new issues identified from the larger literature on teaching and learning and faculty work in the past decade. Respondents used a 4-point Likert-type scale (1 = *not at all*, 2 = *to a slight extent*, 3 = *to a moderate extent*, and 4 = *to a great extent*) to rate each issue in terms of how it was addressed through their faculty development services. Complete tables of respondents' mean ratings are in Appendix B, arranged by their key areas. This section discusses the issues developers indicated they address the most (Table 4.1) and the institutional differences in developers' responses.

Top Issues Addressed Through Faculty Development Services

The leading issues faculty development centers are providing services for have remained quite consistent when compared with results from a decade ago (Sorcinelli et al., 2006). Developers identified the following five issues their services currently address to a *moderate* or *great extent* (mean = 3.00 or more):

1. New faculty orientation/development, 3.48 (up from 3.03 in 2006)
2. Integrating technology into traditional teaching and learning settings, 3.28 (unchanged from 3.28)
3. Active, inquiry-based, or problem-based learning, 3.25 (up from 3.00)
4. Assessment of student learning outcomes, 3.21 (up from 2.57)
5. Course and curriculum reform, 3.08 (up from 2.40)

Our 2006 study, new faculty development was identified as one of three principal issues for which centers offered services and remains the key issue that centers have sustained or increased services for over the past decade, with a particular focus on new faculty orientation programs. This finding suggests that centers remain attuned and responsive to the need to create a welcoming environment for a new, more diverse generation of faculty (Austin, Sorcinelli, & McDaniels, 2007; Trower, 2012). Research shows that early career faculty report concerns about the extent to which their institutions are collegial and provide welcoming communities (Gappa, Austin, &

TABLE 4.1

Issues Currently Addressed by Faculty Development Services

Category	Service	N	All Mean (SD)	R/D Mean (SD)	Comp Mean (SD)	LA Mean (SD)	CC Mean (SD)	Can Mean (SD)
FWCD	New faculty orientation/development	328	3.48 (.78)	3.41 (.80)	3.43 (.83)	3.55 (.79)	3.77 (.57)	3.63 (.63)
T&L	Integrating technology into "traditional" teaching and learning settings (e.g., clickers)	330	3.28 (.85)	3.26 (.84)	3.28 (.88)	3.39 (.90)	3.13 (.90)	3.41 (.84)
T&L	Active, inquiry-based, or problem-based learning	322	3.25 (.88)	3.29 (.89)	3.08 (1.01)	3.28 (.77)	3.20 (.93)	3.41 (.84)
EII	Assessment of student learning outcomes	329	3.21 (.87)	3.15 (.92)	3.23 (.85)	3.36 (.74)	3.23 (.86)	3.22 (.93)
EII	Course and curriculum reform	324	3.08 (.95)	3.03 (.96)	3.08 (.93)	3.25 (.80)	3.00 (.98)	2.96 (1.15)
T&L	Blended learning approaches	321	2.88 (1.02)	2.93 (1.05)	2.71 (1.04)	2.97 (.98)	2.83 (1.04)	3.07 (1.00)
T&L	Teaching in online and distance environments	326	2.83 (1.10)	2.86 (1.11)	2.69 (1.03)	2.81 (1.09)	2.70 (1.18)	3.08 (1.13)
T&L	Scholarship of teaching and learning (SoTL)	320	2.80 (1.03)	2.77 (1.00)	2.75 (1.00)	2.77 (1.28)	2.66 (1.01)	3.04 (1.04)
FWCD	Mentoring programs for underrepresented faculty	309	2.71 (.80)	2.69 (.81)	2.51 (.72)	2.80 (.81)	2.87 (.73)	2.93 (.87)

FWCD	Orientation and support for part-time/adjunct faculty	317	2.62 (1.05)	2.67 (1.04)	2.78 (1.05)	2.63 (1.10)	2.57 (1.01)	2.17 (.92)
EII	Program assessment (e.g., for accreditation)	321	2.61 (1.10)	2.58 (1.16)	2.72 (1.04)	2.61 (.92)	2.69 (.104)	2.28 (1.17)
FWCD	Orientation and support for fixed-term faculty	299	2.61 (1.10)	2.65 (1.04)	2.62 (1.15)	2.54 (1.29)	2.43 (1.10)	2.56 (1.04)
T&L	Multiculturalism and diversity related to teaching	326	2.60 (.99)	2.75 (1.00)	2.48 (1.05)	2.52 (.91)	2.23 (.77)	2.85 (.864)
FWCD	Midcareer and senior faculty development	318	2.59 (.98)	2.63 (.97)	2.50 (.93)	2.61 (1.15)	2.57 (.94)	2.62 (.94)
T&L	Creating course/teaching portfolios	314	2.50 (1.09)	2.47 (1.08)	2.46 (1.09)	2.65 (1.08)	2.52 (1.15)	2.68 (.95)

Note. FWCD = faculty work and career development; T&L = teaching and learning; EII = educational/institutional improvement; R/D = research/doctoral institutions; Comp = comprehensive institutions; LA = liberal arts colleges; CC = community colleges; Can = Canadian institutions. 1 = *not at all*; 2 = *to a slight extent*; 3 = *to a moderate extent*; 4 = *to a great extent*.

Trice, 2007; Rice, Sorcinelli, & Austin, 2000). New faculty orientation programs provide an initial opportunity for new faculty members to begin to make the collegial connections that can foster their satisfaction and morale (Gappa et al., 2007). Developers also see services dedicated to newcomers as a way to feature teaching and learning as a part of the institution's professional agenda, to introduce new faculty to the teaching center and offerings, and to connect the center to other key university offices (Cook & Kaplan, 2011).

The next three topics—technology, active learning, and assessment—also were among the five most addressed issues identified by developers a decade ago. In the current survey, respondents across all institutional types reported that these issues remain among their highest priorities. In higher education institutions and disciplinary societies, and in the national discourse in higher education, more emphasis is being placed on these key pedagogical issues, as shown by the increase in scholarly research addressing them. In this context, it is encouraging to know that faculty developers continue to direct their efforts toward engaging faculty—from new to senior faculty—in the effective use of technology, active learning, and assessment in the classroom.

Of particular note, both our studies found that developers recognized the critical importance of integrating technology into traditional teaching and learning settings. In our 2006 study, this issue was rated as one of the top three challenges facing faculty (3.51); it also was a top issue addressed by centers (3.28). The current findings suggest that integrating technology remains a critical issue that centers are actively addressing (3.28). In addition, developers reported they are offering services regarding teaching through blended learning approaches at just under "*a moderate extent*" (2.88, a new item) and for teaching in online and distance environments (2.83, up from 2.63). Taken together, these findings indicate that technology remains a very important issue for centers. Faculty developers are offering robust services for incorporating technology into the traditional classroom and, at least to some extent, are supporting the effective use of blended and online learning approaches. Encouragingly, they are not alone in this endeavor. The current survey data, reported in Chapter 2, indicate that center directors are actively collaborating with technology centers (77% reported collaboration at a *moderate* or *great extent*), and that technology centers also offer programming independently (67% reported programming at a *moderate* or *great extent*).

Respondents also indicated they were more aggressively addressing the issue of course and curriculum reform than they were a decade ago. The current mean score of respondents is 3.08, up from a mean of 2.40, moving this issue into one of the uppermost areas centers now address. Many universities and colleges are expanding their educational offerings to include an array of technology-mediated experiences, and the result is a growing need for curricular planning for these new pedagogical approaches. Increasingly, centers have been responding by offering intensive institutes or FLCs on course design (Fink, 2013). Furthermore, administrators of some programs have supported departmental or college-level efforts to conduct curriculum reviews (Cook & Kaplan, 2011).

Other Issues Addressed Through Faculty Development Services

Other important faculty development issues are receiving some programmatic attention. Respondents indicated that the following six issues are addressed by their centers to *"a moderate extent"* (above 2.50): the scholarship of teaching and learning (SoTL; 2.80), mentoring programs for faculty from underrepresented groups (2.71), orientation and support for part-time and adjunct faculty (2.62) as well as orientation and support for fixed-term faculty (2.61), program assessment (e.g., for accreditation; 2.61), multiculturalism and diversity related to teaching (2.60), and midcareer and senior faculty development (2.59; see Table 4.1). We note that three of these issues—program assessment, orientation and support for fixed-term faculty, and midcareer and senior faculty development—were not explored a decade ago but were included in this iteration of the survey because of their currency in the academy at this time.

Among the issues examined in both studies, some appear to have increased in importance, including SoTL (2.80, up from 2.57), mentoring programs for faculty from underrepresented populations (2.71, up from 1.90), and orientation and support for part-time and adjunct faculty (2.62, up from 2.11).

The increase in support services for SoTL responds to a growing body of research indicating that faculty who engage in systematic inquiry on student learning in their own classrooms report a wide range of benefits from that work. Outcomes include greater enthusiasm for teaching, changes in the design of courses, and documented improvements in the quality of their students' learning (Condon, Iverson, Manduca, Rutz, & Willett, 2016; Huber & Hutchings, 2005). The increase in programs for SoTL also aligns with the national and international interest in better understanding how and how much students are learning, and its impact is illustrated by the concomitant increase in faculty development conferences and journals focused on SoTL (Beach, 2015; Kern, Mettetal, Dixson, & Morgan, 2015).

Growing interest at centers in mentoring programs for underrepresented faculty undoubtedly reflects the efforts on many campuses to recruit, develop, and retain a more diverse faculty. Mentoring, formal and informal, is seen as perhaps the most effective method for socializing and supporting new faculty in their careers (Johnson, 2007). Studies suggest that the kind of climate and collegiality women faculty and faculty of color experience on campus is of greatest significance in determining their satisfaction and capacity to succeed (Trower, 2012; Wasburn, 2007; Yun, Baldi, & Sorcinelli, 2016). Similarly, increased interest in part-time and adjunct faculty reflects the rapidly rising proportion of faculty being hired into such positions (Gappa et al., 2007; Kezar, 2012; Kezar & Sam, 2010) and a recognition of their impact on student learning.

Institutional Differences

Across institutional types, the portfolio of services provided is very similar; that is, we did not find significant variation in the relative extent to which various issues are prioritized in program offerings. Some variations, however, deserve mention. The results showed that community colleges and Canadian institutions are providing services concerning teaching in online and distance environments somewhat more than other institutional types. This could reflect the organization of centers in these institutions to include support for these modalities, or it could reflect the relative maturity of such services at the other institutional types. Respondents from community colleges also reported providing more services pertaining to orienting and supporting part-time and adjunct faculty than did other institutions, a finding that is quite understandable given the high percentages of part-time and adjunct faculty employed in community colleges. On the other hand, developers from liberal arts colleges reported providing more services than the other institutions for integrating technology into traditional teaching and learning settings. Liberal arts colleges and Canadian institutions reported providing more mentoring programs for underrepresented faculty than those from other institutional types, as well as more frequently addressing the issue of course and teaching portfolios.

Issues Less Addressed Through Faculty Development Services

Directors identified a number of issues for which they offered services to only *a slight extent* or *not at all*. Within services pertaining to teaching and learning (Appendix B), 4 of 14 issues—community and service-learning, writing across the curriculum, peer review of teaching, and teaching adult learners—had overall means between 2.00 and 2.49, indicating offerings between a *slight* and *moderate extent.* Interestingly, each of these issues had a mean above 2.50 for Canadian institutions. Overall, the mean responses concerning the extent of offering services for all teaching and learning issues were higher for Canadian institutions than those of other institutional types. Two issues— team teaching and sustainability across the curriculum—fell below a mean of 2.00 overall, indicating they were addressed by centers to a slight extent or not at all. We speculate that institutions are unlikely to encourage team teaching under most circumstances to optimize the use of faculty time. Thus, center staff probably would be less likely to direct resources to this topic than to other needs. Sustainability is a burgeoning focus for many universities, as shown by the increasing number of member institutions (almost 900 internationally) in the American Association of Sustainability in Higher Education. These institutions submit voluntary reports on their sustainability initiatives in academics, engagement, operations, and planning and administration for recognition that spans bronze to platinum levels (see https://stars.aashe.org). It is still a new enough university focus, however, to be unfamiliar to many of the developers.

Several issues pertaining to faculty work and career development were not generally addressed through services (see Appendix B). Four issues— teaching assistant development, tenure and promotion preparation, scholarly writing, and leadership development for faculty—rated between 2.00 and 2.33, indicating they are addressed by centers *to a slight extent.* Six issues had means below 2.00, indicating they were not addressed at all: ethical conduct of faculty work, international faculty development, preparing future faculty, posttenure review, time management, and sabbatical planning. All these issues reflect the multiple and changing roles of faculty, which was identified as a key challenge for faculty, faculty developers, and higher education institutions in our earlier study. Our current findings suggest that colleges and universities are still grappling with the question of how to best support faculty in all the roles they are asked to fulfill. Institutional leaders may also be recognizing that faculty development centers alone cannot handle the many issues of import to faculty work, and that some issues must be supported elsewhere in the institution.

Among the eight issues pertaining to educational/institutional improvement, three issues—general education reform, unit and program evaluation, and interdisciplinary collaborations—had means between 2.22 and 2.48 (see Appendix B), indicating at least some services are being directed to these issues. It is worth noting that faculty developers in comprehensive universities and community colleges rated the issue of general education reform above 2.50 (2.54 in comprehensive universities and 2.72 in community colleges). In contrast, in our prior study, the mean rating of general education reform as an issue being addressed by all institutional types was 1.98 (1.95 in comprehensive universities and 2.29 in community colleges); it was among the issues least addressed with services. This finding suggests that in comprehensive universities and community colleges, faculty developers may be working with faculty leaders and administrators in academic affairs (the domains that general education reform is likely to fall under) to provide pedagogical expertise and resources to help with general education course design and redesign. In 2006, we predicted that faculty developers would be increasingly active in general education reform and, to some extent, that prediction is beginning to be borne out.

Finally, two issues—departmental leadership and management (1.92) and faculty and department entrepreneurship (1.38)—are barely being addressed by centers in 2016. In 2006 developers rated the extent to which they addressed departmental leadership at a similarly low level (1.94); however, they rated the need to provide training for departmental leadership and management as quite high (3.10). The department is the locus for a great deal of the work of a university or college; the department chair serves as a critical advocate for a culture of teaching and faculty professional development (Buller, 2012). Perhaps even more important, research suggests that programs targeting departments (rather than individual faculty members) can provide a powerful strategy for pedagogical improvement (Wieman, Perkins, & Gilbert, 2010). Arguably, the preparation and ongoing support of department chairs, especially in supporting improvement in teaching, is a strategic institutional investment, but it is not being addressed in any robust fashion in many faculty development centers.

In 1975 Bergquist and Phillips proposed three levels for focus in faculty development—instructional, professional/faculty, and organizational. Some 40 years later, scholars in the field have contemplated whether the classic model of the three-legged stool of faculty development still influences the practices of teaching and learning centers and will influence them in the future (Lee, 2010; Sorcinelli, Gray, & Birch, 2011). Our current findings affirm that critical aspects of all three subfields are included in the work of centers. At the same time, faculty developers report that the teaching and learning/ instructional agenda remains the most prominent focus of centers.

Signature Services and Examples

After asking all participants to indicate the extent to which their faculty development programs offer services pertaining to 39 instructional, professional, and organizational issues, we asked which of up to three of those services directors consider the signature services of their centers or programs.

TABLE 4.2
Directors' Signature Services by Institutional Type

Category	Service		Percentage of Directors					
		All	R/D	Comp	LA	CC	Can
FWCD	New faculty orientation/development	36%	32%	36%	33%	43%	50%
T&L	Active, inquiry-based, or problem-based learning	34%	44%	17%	20%	43%	33%
T&L	Integrating technology into traditional teaching and learning settings (e.g., clickers)	28%	35%	22%	20%	21%	25%
EII	Course and curriculum reform	21%	22%	22%	27%	7%	8%
T&L	Scholarship of teaching and learning (SoTL)	18%	22%	14%	0%	7%	42%
EII	Assessment of student learning outcomes	17%	23%	11%	13%	21%	0%
T&L	Teaching in online and distance environments	16%	15%	22%	20%	14%	8%
FWCD	Teaching assistant development	10%	6%	19%	13%	0%	17%
T&L	Blended learning approaches	8%	1%	25%	13%	0%	0%
FWCD	Mentoring programs for underrepresented faculty	8%	7%	3%	7%	21%	17%
T&L	Teaching adult learners	7%	7%	0%	7%	14%	17%

Note. N = 155; unreported = 38. FWCD = faculty work and career development; T&L = teaching and learning; EII = educational/institutional improvement; R/D = research/ doctoral institutions; Comp = comprehensive institutions; LA = liberal arts colleges; CC = community colleges; Can = Canadian institutions. The full table is presented in Appendix B.

Table 4.2 presents responses to this inquiry, reporting any issue identified by 15% or more of respondents in any institutional type as a signature service. The full list of ratings is presented in Appendix B.

For all directors across all institutional types, the services that rose to the top as signature were almost identical to those that were individually rated as the services being offered to the greatest extent. Top services identified by at least 20% of directors included new faculty orientation/development (36%); support for active, inquiry-based, or problem-based learning (34%); integrating technology into traditional teaching and learning settings (28%); and course and curriculum reform (21%). Although it was included among the services offered to the greatest extent, assessment of student learning outcomes was identified by only 17% of directors as a signature service. Overall, directors believe that the programs they offer most are also their highest quality and most important programs; in other words, their signature programs.

Phone interviews with directors and developers from a wide range of centers, from small colleges to state systems, yielded a rich set of creative programs. Initiatives may have just started up or been offered continuously for 20 years; the majority have been running for more than 5 years. Several respondents pointed to published articles and conference presentations highlighting these programs.

We offer here several profiles created from the interviews that exemplify the top signature services.

New Faculty Orientation

The College of Lake County Professional Development Center in Illinois has offered a New Adjunct Faculty Orientation prior to each semester since 2002. This full-day program is scheduled for the Saturday prior to orientation week when all faculty return to campus for the semester. The morning session covers an introduction to the community college, vital information from human resources, and a tour of campus that includes brief presentations by staff from resource areas (information technology, the Learning Assistance Center, Office of Students With Disabilities, etc.). The afternoon session focuses on classroom instruction. Participants choose topics for discussion and take part in multiple small-group discussions, rotating among topics to maximize their opportunities to learn from each other.

New York Institute of Technology's Teaching and Learning Center offers a coordinated set of workshops for new and tenure-track faculty, beginning with a one-day new faculty orientation and a set of lunches where participants meet key people at the institution. Also included are sessions with the provost and deans on institutional expectations for tenure and promotion and with near-peers and department chairs on preparation of reappointment, tenure and promotion portfolios, and a session on strategically planning one's career during the tenure-track years.

St. Louis Community College's Professional Development Program offers its new full-time faculty a three-pronged program that includes a five-day paid orientation prior to fall semester, weekly meetings throughout the fall semester, and a four-day intensive teaching institute in the spring.

Integrating Technology and Active Learning

The University of South Dakota's Center for Teaching and Learning's fellow-ship program is an instructive example of institutional attention to support-ing faculty as they develop strategies to use technology effectively in support of active and engaged learning. The center offers a concentrated (two-week) course design and redesign fellowship that promotes best practices in course design, team-based learning, educational technology, and learner-centered teaching. These fellowships help faculty design face-to-face, blended, and online courses. The program accepts 12 to 16 participants each cycle, and all faculty and instructional staff (including graduate assistants) are eligible for this competitive award. Course design fellows receive a stipend, four pedagogical books, and one-on-one technical assistance from the Center for Teaching and Learning staff during the semester they first teach their course. The seminar leaders encourage faculty members to incorporate active learn-ing experiences based on strategic course objectives, and the entire fellowship experience has been built to model such engaged learning.

Course Reform

In the Pennsylvania State System of Higher Education's Developmental Grant Program, proposals may focus on course, program, departmental, or interdisciplinary reforms. The more faculty are involved, the more funding is made available. Twenty-four campuses in the system have access to this grant-funded opportunity, which includes preapplication consultation for the faculty involved. Other center directors described institutes of varying lengths and intensity aimed at course redesign, which are described in more detail in Chapter 5, in the section titled "Signature Approaches."

Institutional Differences

Although each of the top four signature services was chosen by at least 20% of directors from each institutional type, there were a few exceptions (see Table 4.2). Among comprehensive institutions, signature services focused on active, inquiry-based, or problem-based learning did not reach this threshold, nor did services pertaining to course and curriculum reform among community college directors. Overall, directors at each institutional type identified five or six signature services that reached a 20% threshold level. In fact, directors at each institutional type seemed to have two prominent signature services, and there was variation across institutional types on which were considered signature. In research and doctoral universities, directors were most likely to identify active, inquiry-based, or problem-based learning (44%) and integrating technology into traditional teaching and learning settings (35%) as key offerings. In comprehensive universities, new faculty development (36%) and blended learning approaches (25%) were most often identified as signature services. In liberal arts colleges, new faculty development (33%) and course and curricular reform (27%) took the lead as signature services. Community college directors reported equal emphasis on new faculty development (43%) and active, inquiry-based, or problem-based learning (43%). Canadian directors identified new faculty orientation (50%) and SoTL (42%) as their signature programs.

Other interesting variations were evident in the data. Course and curriculum reform was identified as a signature service most often by directors at liberal arts colleges (27%) and much less so by community college directors (7%). Research university directors identified SoTL as a signature service (22%) more often than did directors in any other institutional type except directors of Canadian institutions (42%). In contrast, assessment of student learning was mentioned more frequently as a top signature service by research and doctoral university directors (23%) and community college directors (21%) than by those in other institutional types. Directors in community colleges also identified mentoring programs for underrepresented faculty as a signature service (21%) in contrast to much less mention of it at other types of institutions.

The comprehensive institution directors and liberal arts college directors mentioned services pertaining to teaching in online and distance environments as signature services more frequently (22% and 20%, respectively) than the directors of the other institutional types. Also, services pertaining to blended learning received 25% of mentions of signature services by directors of comprehensive institutions but were mentioned only infrequently by those at other institutional types. In contrast, directors at comprehensive universities were less likely to identify active learning as a signature service (17%).

We note also that the Canadian institutions showed some distinctive responses. Although services related to new faculty development were among the signature services at all institutional types, 50% of Canadian developers identified them. Additionally, as noted already, 42% of Canadian directors identified SoTL as a signature service. These variations in signature services by institutional type are reminders that faculty needs and institutional responses are not the same across all institutions. Institutional contexts, including faculty and student demographics, institutional history, and strategic priorities, shape developers' decisions about the allocation of resources to support faculty needs. This attention to context was affirmed in interviews. Developers most often named the needs of the faculty, needs assessments, and experience over time as influences on the development of their signature programs.

Service Areas Directors Wish to Expand

From the list of 39 teaching and learning, faculty work and career development, and educational/institutional improvement issues facing faculty and institutions (survey items 35, 36, 37; see Appendix A), we asked directors to name up to three services they would add or expand in their portfolio if they were given the opportunity or additional resources. As with the current and signature services, we analyzed responses by institutional type to determine if there were differing priorities among different types of institutions. That approach proved extremely interesting and useful, since patterns of choices differed greatly among research and doctoral and comprehensive unversities, liberal arts and community colleges, and Canadian universities. Table 4.3 presents the results of the analysis, focusing on those areas that garnered at least 15% of choices in any one institutional type as being among the three services they would add or expand.

The top services most frequently mentioned by directors across *all* institutional types as candidates for expansion were midcareer and late-career faculty development and peer review of teaching. Other services were prioritized by directors in particular institutional types: SoTL was the most frequently selected service to add or expand, and mentoring programs for underrepresented faculty, departmental programs to strengthen leadership and management and programs in support of multiculturalism and diversity related to teaching were also identified as priority areas for expansion. The following sections discuss these services and present signature programs related to them from a variety of institutions.

SoTL

SoTL was seen as important to add or expand by research universities, comprehensive universities, and liberal arts colleges, which all rated the issue very highly relative to other services (see Table 4.3). Liberal arts colleges in particular viewed SoTL as a priority for expansion; this topic constituted 43% of the liberal arts college directors' nominations for expanded activities. Liberal

TABLE 4.3

Directors' Services to Add or Expand by Institutional Type

Service Category	Services	Percentage of Directors					
		All	R/D	Comp	LA	CC	Can
T&L	Scholarship of teaching and learning (SoTL)	23%	22%	30%	43%	7%	10%
FWCD	Midcareer and senior faculty development	21%	24%	18%	21%	23%	20%
FWCD	Mentoring programs for underrepresented faculty	17%	19%	15%	0%	31%	20%
EII	Departmental leadership and management	17%	24%	9%	7%	31%	0%
T&L	Peer review of teaching	16%	18%	15%	21%	15%	20%
T&L	Multiculturalism and diversity related to teaching	15%	9%	21%	14%	23%	10%
FWCD	Orientation and support for part-time/adjunct faculty	12%	10%	21%	7%	0%	30%
FWCD	Leadership development for faculty	12%	15%	8%	7%	8%	20%
EII	Assessment of student learning outcomes	12%	13%	12%	14%	8%	20%
FWCD	Scholarly writing	10%	10%	6%	14%	8%	20%
EII	Course and curriculum reform	9%	4%	15%	21%	8%	10%
T&L	Blended learning approaches	7%	6%	3%	0%	8%	20%
EII	General education reform	7%	3%	6%	21%	8%	10%
T&L	Creating course/teaching portfolios	5%	3%	0%	0%	8%	30%

Note. N = 147; unreported = 46. T&L = teaching and learning; FWCD = faculty work and career development; EII = educational/institutional improvement; R/D = research/doctoral universities; Comp = comprehensive universities; LA = liberal arts colleges; CC = community colleges; Can = Canadian institutions. The full table is presented in Appendix B.

arts colleges already address SoTL in their portfolio of services (mean = 2.77; Table 4.1) at a level near *to a moderate extent*, but not a single director in those institutions indicated that it was among his or her signature programs. It would be interesting to explore what kinds of conversations about SoTL have taken place at the national level among liberal arts and small-college associations to determine if the level of response to the survey is driven by a larger conversation or by more local preferences of individual directors. Research universities currently support SoTL to a modest extent (mean = 2.77; Table 4.1); at the same time, directors at these institutions still considered it an important service for further expansion. Comprehensive universities viewed SoTL as their top priority for expansion, with 30% of their directors choosing it. They also indicated some current attention to SoTL but identified other services that they believe define their signature programs. Support for SoTL does not appear to be among the services that community colleges offer or that directors in that institutional climate feel a press to add or expand (only 7% of directors identified it for expansion). Canadian institutions also did not frequently nominate SoTL for expansion (10%), perhaps because they are already highly engaged in SoTL activities. In fact, Canadian universities indicated a reasonable focus on SoTL among their current services (mean = 3.04; Table 4.1) and a high-level focus on SoTL among their signature programs, with 42% of directors identifying it. Clearly, there is both national and international interest in deeper engagement in SoTL. The following are examples of centers that have signature programs in support of SoTL.

Indiana University's Center for Innovative Teaching and Learning's SoTL program is now in its 13th year. One of the most important goals of the program is to foster significant, long-lasting learning for all students while simultaneously bringing recognition and reward to instructors who practice evidence-based teaching. Each year, a Community of Inquiry composed of about 8 to 10 SoTL fellows meets on a monthly basis to systematically analyze evidence of student learning, situate fellows' work within the existing literature, and collaborate with other faculty in or across disciplines. Following their fellowship year, fellows contribute to the body of knowledge about teaching and learning by disseminating their research findings through local, national, and international venues. Over the past year, the program has funded Student Learning Analytics Fellows who are conducting faculty-driven research projects using learning analytics to foster student engagement, retention, and success. Each SoTL project receives $2,000 in research funds. The program also hosts some 10 campuswide events each year and provides a variety of local resources to SoTL scholars (e.g., resources in the offices of assessment, research, and the registrar) as they go about conducting research in traditional and virtual classrooms. The program's website also features a selective list of the SoTL work that has been conducted at the campus in Bloomington since 1999.

Stonehill College's Center for Teaching & Learning has offered an annual, multiday, overnight writing retreat devoted to SoTL since 2010. In addition to workshops on SoTL methods and project design, the retreat provides faculty members with opportunities to share their work with colleagues as well as free time for writing. Faculty members developing new SoTL projects and those working on writing about their SoTL findings are encouraged to apply. The retreat is held annually at an off-campus retreat center, and meals and lodging are provided.

Midcareer and Senior Faculty Development

The one service that developers in all institutional types agreed on as uniformly important to expand was midcareer and late-career faculty development (21%; Table 4.3). The prominence of midcareer and senior-career faculty development as a key service developers would like to add or expand indicates the urgency of the need to address faculty vitality across the career span. Reports indicate that at some colleges and universities, as many as one in three professors are age 60 and older (Baldwin & Zeig, 2013). This increase in the proportion of senior faculty raises the following question: What are institutions doing to support midcareer and senior faculty? Although many teaching and faculty development centers have long histories of focusing their efforts and resources on supporting early career faculty, most have directed less attention on midcareer and late-career professors. However, the following example illustrates one approach.

Wake Forest University's Teaching and Learning Center offers an annual Graylyn Teaching Renewal Retreat for Advanced Career Faculty. The goal of the retreat is to offer advanced career faculty an opportunity to explore new paths, pedagogical and personal, in an effort to reconnect them with the excitement that originally led them into teaching careers. The three-day retreat is scheduled in early summer and brings together 20 to 25 faculty members from a variety of disciplines and universities in and outside North Carolina. The director of the teaching center works with other center directors to create the workshops and facilitate the working groups. Each school pays for its own faculty participants, which makes the program sustainable.

Mentoring Programs for Underrepresented Faculty

Mentoring programs for underrepresented faculty were identified by 17% of directors as a service to expand (Table 4.3). However, the level of interest in this focus varied considerably by institutional type; although not a single liberal arts director identified it, between 15% and 31% of directors at other institutional types did name this among their top services to expand.

Community colleges in particular (31%) may want to match the diversity of their faculty to the diversity of their student bodies, which encompass adult learners, students from different racial and ethnic backgrounds, and students who come to college with extremely diverse levels of preparations. One might speculate that creating mentoring programs is particularly challenging at community colleges, where a large proportion of the faculty typically work in part-time positions. A range of approaches to mentoring is emerging across the country, including group mentoring and networks that serve mentoring functions, in addition to more traditional one-on-one models. The following is an example of an innovative approach.

University of Massachusetts Amherst's Center for Teaching and Faculty Development has created Mutual Mentoring, a campuswide initiative for new, early career, and underrepresented faculty members. The core of the Mutual Mentoring initiative is a network-based mentoring model in which faculty work with multiple mentors who provide support in their areas of expertise rather than a single mentor who is less likely to be able to address the variety of challenges faced by diverse teacher scholars. The model is operationalized through team and micro grants that empower early career faculty to create robust networks of mentoring partners to support their context-sensitive needs, which include getting started, excelling at teaching and research, career advancement, and managing work-life responsibilities. An evaluation of the program over a seven-year period found that women and faculty of color were overrepresented in the initiative because the network-based mentoring model provided the type of nonhierarchical, relational, and reciprocal mentoring structure desired by these populations. In addition, faculty members who participated in the initiative were more likely to regard mentoring as a career-enhancing activity as well as to develop mutually beneficial mentoring partnerships than were their nonparticipating peers (Jung, Baldi, & Sorcinelli, 2016). Going forward, the program has expanded the pool of eligible beneficiaries to include full-time lecturers and posttenure faculty, an acknowledgment of the need for mentoring at all ranks and stages of the faculty career.

Departmental Leadership and Management

Programs in support of departmental leadership and management were identified by 17% of directors for expansion, but the primary support for these activities came from directors at research universities (24%) and community colleges (31%; Table 4.3). Although historically centers for teaching and faculty development have not included leadership development, the need for good leadership, especially at the departmental level, is gaining traction at many institutions. Department chairs and deans are at the crossroads and front lines of organizational change, such as efforts to improve learning and teaching. Most of those who assume these leadership positions are experts in disciplinary areas and have not had formal management or leadership preparation. As the challenges affecting higher education institutions increase, institutional leaders need support, preparation, and training. We expect more institutions will include leadership preparation in the portfolios of their faculty development centers or will find ways to share this responsibility across multiple units. The following is an example of institutional programming in this area.

Michigan State University has included leadership development as a responsibility of its Faculty and Organizational Development Office for many years. The opportunities offered are extensive, including seminars and workshops for institutional leaders at all levels. For example, about once a month, all institutional leaders, including deans, chairs, and unit directors, have the opportunity to participate in the Leadership and Administrator Seminar Series, involving a three-hour workshop focused on leadership skills or key institutional issues of relevance to institutional leaders. The workshops have served as a vehicle for creating a sense of connection and an invisible network of collegiality among leaders across campus so that each person in a leadership role knows to whom to turn for advice and support. The leadership development portfolio also includes cohort programs offered over the course of months (including the Academic Leadership Program offered in conjunction with other institutions in the Council of Inter-Institutional Collaboration). Other activities include leadership learning communities and individual consultations.

Peer Review of Teaching

Peer review of teaching was the only other issue that ranked among the top choices for addition or expansion of services across all institutional types (16%; Table 4.3). However, it did not rank at all among the top issues for which centers currently offer services or among the signature services reported by directors, so attention to this issue would represent a new direction for most teaching and faculty development centers. A few institutions had peer review activities among their signature programs, as indicated in the following example.

Western Michigan University's Office of Faculty Development (OFD) offers faculty confidential peer observation and feedback. All the peer observers are faculty members from a range of disciplines who have been recognized for teaching excellence. They are recruited and trained in a developmental approach to peer observation that involves initial consultation, observation, survey and discussion with students in the class, and then feedback and recommendations. Faculty can choose particular elements of their teaching they would like feedback on and can choose observers from a menu on the OFD's website that notes areas of expertise among the trained observers. The center arranges the initial meeting and provides support for compiling student surveys, but the observation pair collaborates on the details of the process, and the feedback and recommendations are given only to the requesting faculty member to use as he or she wishes.

Multiculturalism and Diversity Related to Teaching

Multiculturalism and diversity related to teaching was identified by 15% of directors for expansion across most institutional types (Table 4.3). In comprehensive institutions, 21% of directors support expanding this focus. At community colleges, 23% of directors support expansion. Recognition is growing that the challenges facing this country and the broader international community require the talents of the full range of the population. Enhanced attention to programs that support multiculturalism and diversity in regard to teaching and learning processes is likely to stay on the horizon for directors as they establish priorities for moving forward. Although services in this area were not among the top signature programs, many institutions are striving to enhance their attention to the learning needs of a diverse population of students. The following example represents a model of excellence.

At Duquesne University, the Center for Teaching Excellence (CTE) works to educate students in an environment that is socially just and to provide opportunities for cross-cultural learning on campus and beyond. CTE weaves this focus throughout its faculty resources and programming by examining the intersections of diversity and pedagogy in CTE workshops, panel discussions, online references, and resources offered through the campus library. For example, recent CTE events have included a workshop titled "Exploring Race and Pedagogy at our Predominantly White University," led by several faculty members, and a discussion titled "Using High-Impact Practices to Improve Learning Outcomes for Underserved Students," facilitated by a faculty member and the director of the CTE. The CTE also developed and posted its own quick tips for promoting diversity in university teaching and linked to online resources on higher education and diversity in terms of race/ethnicity, sexuality/gender, religious diversity, social class, environmental issues, and women.

Institutional Differences

As noted throughout this discussion of expansion areas, individual institutional types varied to a noticeable extent in the services directors felt important to add to their portfolios if they had more opportunities and resources. Again, we considered there was a noteworthy consensus about the value of an issue when it received support from 15% of directors as one of the top three areas identified for expansion. As shown in Table 4.3, research universities identified leadership as an area for expansion in center activities, specifically departmental leadership (24%) and leadership development for faculty (15%). Comprehensive universities identified orientation and support for part-time instructors (21%) and course and curriculum reform (15%) as areas for growth. Liberal arts college directors indicated a focus on creating a more coherent undergraduate program through course and curriculum reform (21%) and general education reform (21%). Community college directors shared their interest in departmental leadership and management (31%) with research university colleagues (24%). Although the percentages are somewhat different, they represent top areas of expansion at both types of institutions. As noted previously, community college directors were more interested in mentoring programs for underrepresented students and multiculturalism and diversity related to teaching and learning than the other types of institutions. Canadian universities had an ambitious list of programs they would add to their portfolios, which included orientation and support for part-time faculty (30%) and creating course and teaching portfolios (30%), as well as several services that reached the threshold of consensus with at least 15% of directors identifying them for expansion: leadership development for faculty, peer review of teaching, assessment of student learning outcomes, scholarly writing, and blended learning approaches.

Although variation across all institutional types was considerable, there was consensus among directors about the value in expanding services concerning midcareer faculty development and peer review of teaching. Additionally, agreement was strong concerning the importance of and interest in expanding services concerning the SoTL, mentoring programs for underrepresented faculty members, departmental leadership and management, and multiculturalism and diversity related to teaching. Higher education watchers can identify various national conversations reflected in these choices. Clearly, faculty development directors are tapped into the current landscape of higher education as well as the presses and priorities of their own institutions.

Although the POD Network's revised mission statement now reads that the organization "is devoted to improving teaching and learning in higher education" (POD Network, n.d.), it is noteworthy that center directors identified as many areas for expansion in faculty work and career development services as they did in teaching and learning services. Educational and institutional improvement does not figure prominently in expansion areas, with the important exception of departmental leadership and management. Taken as a whole, these findings suggest that center administrators will always need to vary their practices and programs depending on the particular missions and needs of their institutions and the interests and expertise of their staff. The findings also suggest that while the subfield of teaching and instructional development is most prominent in faculty development, it would be a mistake to think that issues of faculty work, career development, and educational improvement will or should ever fully recede from the portfolios of centers. They are in fact among the issues developers see as emergent and in need of serious consideration in the field.

Equally interesting are those services that are not identified by developers as uppermost priorities for expansion, even if the centers were given the opportunity and resources to expand. Directors did not identify any of their most offered services or their signature services as needing expansion. The services mentioned as most important to develop or extend are not being addressed currently.

Conclusion

The apparent stability in services offered over the past decade points to enduring priorities such as developing new faculty and responding to the continued and burgeoning interest in technology, assessment, and evidence-based practices in teaching and learning. But a singular focus on these leading priorities may obscure a diverse set of offerings among different institutional types that are specific to their missions, faculty profiles, and student bodies. Developers remain committed to addressing core issues, especially in teaching and learning and faculty work and career development, and have a clear vision for those services they would expand, which include greater variety in each of these two areas.

Chapter Highlights

- The core issues faculty development programs address by providing services remain quite consistent when compared with data from a decade ago. We did not find significant variation in the relative extent to which issues are prioritized in program offerings across different types of institutions.
- Leading issues currently addressed by centers are new faculty development; integrating technology into traditional teaching and learning settings; active, inquiry-based, or problem-based learning;

assessment of student learning outcomes; and course and curricular reform.

- For directors across all institutional types, the services that rose to the top as signature are almost identical to those individually rated as the services being offered to the greatest extent.

- The primary issue for which developers across all institutional types most wish to expand services is midcareer and late-career faculty development. They also agreed they would like to offer more resources for peer review of teaching. Research universities, comprehensive universities, and liberal arts colleges all rated SoTL very highly for expansion relative to other services.

- Other services directors indicated they would most like to add or expand, given the resources to do so, included mentoring programs for underrepresented faculty, especially in community colleges and Canadian universities. Adding programs for departmental leadership and management was particularly important to research universities and community colleges. Directors at community colleges and comprehensive institutions were also interested in expanding services that address multiculturalism and diversity related to teaching.

5

OUR APPROACHES TO
FACULTY DEVELOPMENT

In Chapter 4, we identified the services developers believe are most important to offer through their teaching centers; that is, topics in the areas of teaching and learning, faculty work and career development, and educational or institutional improvement addressed by formal programming. The pattern of findings suggests, overall, that the key services offered most by developers have remained constant over the past decade. In this study, we wanted to examine more deeply the approaches faculty developers use to offer services to their campuses; that is, the mix of workshops, consultations, institutes, courses, learning communities, and other vehicles they use to address faculty development topics.

To explore these approaches, we created a set of questions parallel to the questions we asked about services (discussed in Chapter 4). We first asked all respondents the extent to which their centers currently use each of 15 approaches in the faculty development literature (Chism, Holley, & Harris, 2012; Gillespie & Robertson, 2010; Hines, 2009). Using a 4-point Likert-type scale (1 = *not at all*, 2 = *to a slight extent*, 3 = *to a moderate extent*, and 4 = *to a great extent*), developers were asked to indicate the extent to which an approach is used as a means for delivering services. We then asked center directors to identify up to three approaches they considered to be their center's signature approaches. Finally, directors selected the topmost approaches they would add or expand in their portfolio if given the resources and opportunity to do so. This chapter presents the findings from these items and discusses the relative impact of different approaches and practices.

Current Approaches to Providing Faculty Development Services

Table 5.1 provides the data concerning the extent to which developers use various approaches to provide faculty development services. Overall, across

75

TABLE 5.1
Approaches Currently Used to Provide Faculty Development Services

Approaches	N	All Mean (SD)	R/D Mean (SD)	Comp Mean (SD)	LA Mean (SD)	CC Mean (SD)	Can Mean (SD)
Hands-on workshops (1–3 hours)	310	3.40 (.81)	3.38 (.80)	3.40 (.82)	3.55 (.72)	3.59 (.57)	3.40 (.82)
Individual consultations	311	3.25 (.93)	3.20 (.99)	3.34 (.80)	3.06 (.89)	3.67 (.62)	3.44 (.96)
Web-based resources (e.g., links to articles or Internet content)	305	3.09 (.94)	3.09 (.94)	3.05 (.92)	3.24 (.91)	3.04 (.94)	3.12 (.93)
Informal discussions with colleagues about teaching problems and solutions over coffee or lunch	307	2.82 (.94)	2.83 (.93)	2.69 (.88)	2.73 (.87)	3.19 (1.11)	2.84 (.99)
Department/discipline-specific workshops (on demand)	307	2.75 (1.01)	2.71 (1.07)	2.81 (.96)	2.87 (1.01)	2.78 (.93)	2.84 (1.03)
Seminars (multiple meeting commitment)	301	2.74 (1.06)	2.64 (1.09)	2.71 (1.10)	3.11 (.88)	2.96 (.98)	2.60 (1.16)
Teaching observation and feedback with a trained consultant	299	2.65 (1.09)	2.62 (1.12)	2.76 (.99)	2.66 (.97)	2.58 (1.17)	2.52 (1.19)
Faculty and professional learning communities (i.e., full semester or academic year, regular meetings)	301	2.62 (1.18)	2.55 (1.15)	2.67 (1.25)	2.72 (1.28)	2.62 (1.20)	2.76 (1.13)
Institutes/retreats (2–3 full days)	297	2.47 (1.17)	2.53 (1.13)	2.40 (1.22)	2.69 (1.07)	2.24 (1.23)	2.32 (1.28)
Structured discussions focused around a reading provided prior to the meeting (e.g., Journal Club)	299	2.46 (1.10)	2.49 (1.11)	2.34 (1.16)	2.37 (1.03)	2.65 (.94)	2.71 (1.12)

Peer observation of teaching with feedback	295	2.25 (1.02)	2.27 (1.02)	2.18 (1.02)	2.11 (1.07)	2.33 (1.11)	2.32 (1.03)
SGID	280	2.12 (1.19)	2.10 (1.22)	2.06 (1.02)	2.33 (1.30)	2.08 (1.22)	2.24 (1.33)
Webinars (1- to 2-hour synchronous Web-based seminars that can be saved and viewed later)	296	2.08 (1.07)	2.14 (1.11)	1.98 (1.07)	2.07 (.98)	1.96 (1.02)	1.84 (1.11)
Electronic newsletter	284	2.06 (1.16)	2.05 (1.14)	2.22 (1.18)	1.78 (1.12)	2.29 (1.30)	2.08 (1.28)
Asynchronous online programs	290	1.84 (1.00)	1.94 (1.06)	1.73 (.91)	1.86 (.93)	1.68 (.90)	1.67 (.92)
Other	66	2.56 (1.25)	2.56 (1.27)	2.64 (1.15)	2.80 (1.64)	3.00 (1.00)	2.00 (1.41)

Note. 1 = *not at all*; 2 = *to a slight extent*; 3 = *to a moderate extent*; and 4 = *to a great extent*. SGID = small-group instructional diagnosis; R/D = research/doctoral institutions; Comp = comprehensive institutions; LA = liberal arts colleges; CC = community colleges; Can = Canadian institutions.

all institutional types, developers identified three primary methods they use to deliver their services: short, hands-on workshops (a mean score of 3.40 on the 1-to-4 scale); individual consultations (3.25); and Web-based resources, such as links to articles or Internet content (3.09). Developers employ another five methods at a *moderate extent*: informal discussions with colleagues about teaching issues (2.82), department/discipline-specific workshops (2.75), seminars with multiple meetings (2.74), teaching observation and feedback with a trained consultant (2.65), and faculty learning communities (FLCs) that extend over a semester or academic year (2.62).

Developers are less likely to use approaches such as multiday, intensive institutes or retreats (2.47), structured discussions focused on a reading or book (2.46), and peer observation of teaching with feedback (2.25). Finally, approaches such as small-group instructional diagnosis (SGID; 2.12), Webinars (2.08), electronic newsletters (2.06), and asynchronous online programs (1.84) are least likely to have taken hold. Developers are markedly uniform in their approaches, and responses offer very few meaningful differences across institutional types.

These rankings give reason to pause. The approaches used to the greatest extent—1- to 3-hour workshops, individual consultation, and Web-based resources—have different affordances for developers and their clients. All are efficient for busy faculty. Workshops can be efficient for developers seeking to reach as many faculty members as possible in a documentable way. Web-based resources can be efficient for faculty, allowing just-in-time access to materials; however, they are challenging for developers to create. Consultations are not efficient for developers, given their one-on-one format, but they are highly valued by developers and faculty for their confidential, relational, and focused nature. The positive news is that these approaches can capture faculty interest, provide them with ideas about new teaching approaches, and encourage them to consider more intensive interventions. However, a workshop, a single consultation, or a website link alone is less likely to provide the sustained support needed as instructors strive to change aspects of their work, for example, when they are incorporating new approaches into their teaching (Chism et al., 2012; Henderson, Beach, & Finkelstein, 2011; Nasmith & Steinert, 2001).

Another point of interest is that the top two approaches are carried out face-to-face rather than virtually, although each approach could be aided by technology. In fact, of the 15 approaches presented, 11 of them engage faculty in dialogue face-to-face; the three lowest ranked approaches engage faculty through technology (i.e., webinars, electronic newsletters, asynchronous online programs). Although we live and work in increasingly technology-driven academic environments, these findings confirm that developers still favor approaches that facilitate peer or consultant connections. They do see the value of Web-based resources (the third most-used approach, with a mean of 3.09), possibly recognizing the ease of use for busy faculty members.

It is also of note that a growing body of scholarship finds greater impacts associated with approaches developers currently use only at a *slight* to *moderate extent*—FLCs, intensive institutes with follow-up support, and workshop series. These approaches are more likely to provide the environments that advance teaching knowledge and behaviors, increase faculty understanding of how students learn, and foster long-term change in a faculty member's instructional choices (Austin, 2011; Beach & Cox, 2004, 2009; Beach, Henderson, & Finkelstein, 2012; Henderson et al., 2011; Ho, Watkins, & Kelly, 2001; Mårtensson, Roxå, & Olsson, 2011; Trigwell, 2012).

Signature Approaches

Table 5.2 provides summary results of the responses directors provided when asked about the signature approaches at their institutions. Because each respondent was asked to identify up to three signature approaches, the percentages in the table reflect the percentage of directors who named the approach among their top choices.

Faculty development directors identified a range of approaches they consider to be signature approaches for delivering services. However, two approaches stood out as most frequently mentioned: hands-on workshops ranging from 1 to 3 hours (which 59% of directors named among their top three) and individual consultations (which 53% named). Several interesting institutional differences emerged. Research and comprehensive universities did not have any signature approaches beyond their top two (workshops and consultations) that garnered more than 25% of directors' support. In addition to identifying hands-on workshops (69%) and individual consultations (39%), liberal arts college directors identified FLCs as a signature approach (54%) far more than did directors at other types of institutions. Liberal arts college directors also identified informal discussions as a signature approach (31%), as did a similar percentage of the Canadian directors (33%). Perhaps learning communities and informal discussions are particularly preferred approaches at liberal arts colleges where faculty members have a history of self-organizing development opportunities and may know each other well enough to readily enjoy in-depth conversations about how their teaching influences student learning.

Although hands-on workshops and individual consultations were mentioned most frequently by directors in all institutional types, directors at community colleges included workshops among their top three signature

TABLE 5.2

Directors' Signature Approaches by Institutional Type

Approaches	All	R/D	Comp	LA	CC	Can
Hands-on workshops (1–3 hours)	59%	64%	59%	69%	46%	50%
Individual consultations	53%	57%	56%	39%	31%	58%
Faculty learning communities (i.e., full semester or academic year, regular meetings)	26%	22%	21%	54%	31%	17%
Department/discipline-specific workshops (on demand)	20%	21%	21%	8%	23%	17%
Informal discussions with colleagues about teaching problems and solutions over coffee or lunch	20%	19%	12%	31%	23%	33%
Institutes/retreats (2–3 full days)	20%	18%	21%	23%	15%	25%
Web-based resources (e.g., links to articles or Internet content)	16%	16%	21%	15%	15%	8%
Seminars (multiple-meeting commitment)	16%	9%	21%	15%	31%	25%
Structured discussions focused around a reading provided prior to the meeting (e.g., Journal Club)	13%	15%	15%	8%	8%	8%
SGID	12%	13%	3%	8%	31%	8%

Note. N = 148; unreported = 45. SGID = small-group instructional diagnosis; R/D = research/doctoral institutions; Comp = comprehensive institutions; LA = liberal arts colleges; CC = community colleges; Can = Canadian institutions.

approaches much less frequently (46%) than those at other institutional types. They mentioned FLCs, seminars, and SGIDs in equal numbers (31%) as signature approaches. In terms of individual consultations, directors at liberal arts colleges and community colleges named this approach much less frequently (39% and 31%, respectively) when identifying their top approaches than did their counterparts at research and doctoral institutions (57%), comprehensive institutions (56%), or Canadian institutions (58%).

Overall, Web-based resources constituted only 16% of the nominations for signature approaches. This is in contrast to the finding that Web-based resources are among the top services offered (as indicated in Table 5.1). Perhaps developers perceive that having such resources available online is expected but not innovative or important enough to rank as a signature approach. Of note also, structured discussions on readings (1.10) and SGIDs (2.12) were neither frequently cited as signature services nor offered on campuses very often (see in Table 5.1).

Through our follow-up phone interviews with participants, we were able to explore the details of some of their signature approaches. Interestingly, very few directors offered details about the two approaches they used most frequently and identified most as signature approaches: short, onetime workshops and individual consultations. Instead, in interviews, they generally chose to discuss approaches they felt were more distinctive. The following descriptions illustrate approaches (other than hands-on workshops and individual consultations, which are rather ubiquitous) that directors identified among their institution's signature approaches. They are presented in the order of their frequency of mention among the top three signature approaches, indicated in Table 5.2.

FLCs

FLCs often consist of a cross-disciplinary community of faculty engaged in a collaborative, long-term curriculum focused on enhancing and assessing undergraduate learning with frequent activities that promote their own learning and development or SoTL. In a twist on this familiar FLC approach, the Center for Teaching and Learning at Chabot College, one of California's community colleges, offers faculty inquiry groups (FIGs), which are not organized around a project or knowledge set as FLCs tend to be, but around a teaching- and learning-related research question. This program evolved from a statewide initiative, the Faculty Inquiry Network, that brought together community college faculty from across California. The FIGs provide the structure needed to bring together the knowledge and experience of faculty to seek solutions to students' learning needs.

One of the initiators was an English instructor who was conducting research in conjunction with the institutional research office, investigating why students who are passing a course drop out or stop attending classes. Although the usual target audience of the FIGs is faculty members, a few groups have involved some staff members; for example, the online retention group includes instructional designers who provide training support to faculty. Other active investigations focus on habits of mind of a healthy student and creating classroom engagement. Many FIGs also engage undergraduate students as coinquirers, thus integrating the student voice into the conversation. The students' work takes a variety of forms, including participating in FIG discussions, creating and presenting student surveys, and making videos for presentation to faculty and staff.

Discipline-specific programs
The Center for Teaching and Learning at Mercer University, which encompasses the Macon, Atlanta, and Savannah campuses in Georgia, works directly with departments, programs, schools, and colleges by offering unit-specific services as a key part of the center's portfolio. Examples of unit-specific projects have included teaching support for departments or programs such as designing and implementing ways to evaluate teaching effectiveness, facilitating peer observation in a department, understanding and using student course evaluation data, exploring and implementing research on particular pedagogies relevant to a discipline, and assisting part-time and adjunct instructors with teaching and course design. Departmental learning support projects have included assessing student learning in a course, department, or program, and rethinking classroom configurations. The center also offers curricular support to departments or schools such as redesigning a major or minor; creating and linking the unit's teaching objectives to course design, assignments, and teaching practices; and analyzing grades over time to detect trends.

Informal discussions with colleagues
The Teaching and Learning Center at the University of the Sciences in Philadelphia offers an informal discussion series called Table Talks that is open to the whole campus and offered twice weekly at consistent times and places. Topics focus on teaching and learning, current trends in higher education, controversial issues facing the campus, and general education. Some faculty use this as an opportunity to present SoTL work, and student affairs staff may present and discuss issues such as the Family Educational Rights and Policy Act (FERPA), the student conduct process, and the institution's honor

code. The director makes a policy of accepting all offers to present, in an effort to work with as many other units of the campus as possible. There is no formal assessment of the impact of the program, but the campus has adopted the name Table Talk for any informal, discussion-oriented event, even if it isn't associated with the series or even the Teaching and Learning Center. Deans have indicated that just seeing topics announced raises consciousness about current ideas and trends in higher education.

Institutes and retreats

The University of Vermont's Writing in the Disciplines Program offers a four-day Writing in the Disciplines Institute to support faculty who are developing or revising an undergraduate course in a major that includes a significant writing component. The goal of the institute is to integrate writing into an undergraduate course in ways that enhance student learning. The institute is widely inclusive in terms of the types of courses that are addressed; faculty come to it with senior seminars, large and small classes, and first-year classes in mind. The only requirement is participants' interest in how writing works in their courses to help students deal with disciplinary material. Designed as a retreat, the program includes readings, brief presentations mixed in with interactive activities (e.g., think/pair/share, a gallery walk of ideas), and stretches of time when people can sit quietly and work on their own materials. Participants are able to share work with colleagues and create assignments and assessments appropriate for their own disciplines. They receive resource materials, good food, and a $750 professional development fund to support implementation of Writing in the Disciplines in their courses. They also share their work with colleagues during the following academic year.

Web-based resources

Oberlin College's Center for Teaching Innovation and Excellence has created a dynamic website that provides access to a wide variety of teaching resources online and allows discussions on teaching-related issues in blog format. The center director posts an Article of the Week for all faculty members as well as an audience that includes individuals outside the college. The overarching goal of the Article of the Week is to combine the collective experience of Oberlin's instructors and the growing body of scholarly literature on teaching to help faculty grapple with their own teaching issues as well as the broader challenges that faculty face as educators. This resource is in its seventh year, and has evolved from a mailed hard-copy format to a blog (languages.oberlin.edu/blogs/ctie) that allows follow-up questions and comments, creating an ongoing dialogue among instructors and center staff. The blog incorporates links to other print and visual materials but requires original writing rather than reprints of copyrighted material. The director spends

8 to 10 hours preparing each article but can adapt reviews of topics to the college's particular culture.

Seminars in a series of multiple meetings

Carleton College's Perlman Center for Teaching and Learning hosts weekly lunch seminars, a program that began some 20 years ago and that became a weekly occurrence about 15 years ago. This faculty-driven and flexible program offers a wide range of topics, so there is a broad audience. In response to a call for proposals at the beginning of each term, faculty use an online suggestion form to submit ideas for the topics of the weekly luncheons. At each of the eight to nine lucheons scheduled per quarter (25 to 26 per year), participants receive lunch and hear a brief presentation followed by conversation. The program serves an average of 41 participants per session, with 1,162 participants in total during the 2014–2015 academic year.

Structured discussions on readings

The Center for Excellence in Teaching and Learning at the University of Wisconsin–Oshkosh organizes a book club that has been offered each semester for the past six years. The club provides an opportunity for a group of 5 to 10 faculty members to read a book focusing on provocative issues related to teaching, learning, and educational matters. The center staff reviews highly regarded and award-winning books on teaching and learning, polls faculty members about possible options, manages the logistics of meeting times and rooms, and purchases a book for each member of the club. This small group of cross-disciplinary colleagues then gets together to talk, share members' successes and struggles, and develop new skills and knowledge. The club usually meets for an hour or so, four or five times during the semester. Participants report multiple benefits from this kind of structured discussion over a compelling book. The gatherings provide intellectual stimulus and personal interactions in a group context; reflection on and interaction with a strong diversity of perspectives; continuous teaching development; and, in the words of one participant, an opportunity to "get out of our nooks and silos and reconnect with colleagues across the community in live, face-to-face conversation—something we all need more of!" Past book choices include *Between the World and Me* (Coates, 2015); *Teaching Naked: How Moving Technology Out of Your Classroom Will Improve Student Learning* (Bowen, 2012); *How Learning Works: Seven Research-Based Principles for Smart Teaching* (Ambrose, Bridges, DiPietro, Lovett, & Norman, 2010); and *Whistling Vivaldi: How Stereotypes Affect Us and What We Can Do (Issues of Our Time)* (Steele, 2011).

SGID

The Center for Faculty Innovation at James Madison University chose its midsemester student feedback technique, Teaching Analysis Poll, as the one initiative it would offer if only allowed a single program in its portfolio. The goal of the program is to provide instructors with rich and meaningful feedback from their students regarding the learning environment in a course. The program is open to all full- and part-time faculty, and early career faculty in particular are drawn to it. This approach is unique in that the center's staff has developed a cadre of faculty peer consultants (rather than staff or students), designated as faculty associates, to attend class, collect and analyze the students' feedback, and meet with the instructor to discuss the students' responses to the course. The program serves about 90 participants per semester, consisting of 75 new and several returning instructors. The program not only is well regarded among faculty but also has significant champions among the college deans, provost, and university president. As an added benefit of the service and approach, the center has documented the program impact on instructors' teaching knowledge and behaviors as well as on student learning.

Approaches Directors Wish to Expand

A review of the approaches directors would either add to their portfolios or expand is provided in Table 5.3. The data indicate significant alignment across institutional types in the top two choices for expansion. FLCs are the primary choice overall (43% of directors identify this as an area for expansion) and in every institutional type (ranging from 36% to 50%). Institutes of two or more days follow the same pattern in the number two position (29% of directors overall, ranging by institutional type from 27% to 39%). Another approach, peer observation of teaching, has strong interest in research universities (25% of directors) and in comprehensive universities (27%). Asynchronous online programs also are of particular interest to research universities (30%). Department and discipline-specific workshops were frequently selected as approaches to expand by directors at Canadian institutions (36%) and comprehensive universities (27%) but received lower ratings among research universities (16%), liberal arts colleges (14%), and community colleges (23%).

It is reassuring that the approaches directors wish to add or expand are documented by a growing literature on their positive effects. In a review of the literature on the impact of faculty development activities, Chism and colleagues (2012) found positive outcomes on teaching development associated

TABLE 5.3

Directors' Approaches to Add or Expand by Institutional Type

Approaches	All	R/D	Comp	LA	CC	Can
Faculty and professional learning communities (i.e., full semester or academic year, regular meetings)	43%	43%	42%	50%	39%	36%
Institutes/retreats (2–3 full days)	29%	27%	30%	29%	39%	27%
Peer observation of teaching with feedback	25%	25%	27%	14%	15%	18%
Asynchronous online programs	25%	30%	21%	21%	8%	36%
Department/discipline-specific workshops (on demand)	21%	16%	27%	14%	23%	36%
Teaching observation and feedback with a trained consultant	20%	24%	12%	21%	15%	27%
Webinars (1- to 2-hour synchronous Web-based seminars that can be saved and viewed later)	18%	21%	9%	29%	8%	18%
Web-based resources (e.g., links to articles or Internet content)	17%	15%	18%	21%	23%	9%
SGID	16%	16%	15%	21%	23%	0%
Seminars (multiple-meeting commitment)	15%	18%	18%		15%	9%
Structured discussions focused around a reading provided prior to the meeting (e.g., Journal Club)	14%	13%	18%	14%	8%	9%
Electronic newsletter	12%	15%	9%	14%	0%	27%
Informal discussions with colleagues about teaching problems and solutions over coffee or lunch	11%	12%	15%	14%	0%	9%
Hands-on workshops (1–3 hours)	7%	6%	6%	14%	15%	0%
Individual consultation	6%	3%	6%	14%	15%	0%
Other	3%	3%	6%	0%	0%	9%

Note. N = 146; unreported = 47. SGID = small-group instructional diagnosis; R/D = research/doctoral institutions; Comp = comprehensive institutions; LA = liberal arts colleges; CC = community colleges; Can = Canadian institutions.

with communities of practice, on which FLCs are modeled: "Although there is great variation among these types of activities, the studies document solid gains for participants; some even are able to trace these to impacts on student learning" (p. 137). They also concluded that institutes of one day or more were found to have positive effects on teaching attitudes and changes in teaching practices. In terms of peer observation of teaching with feedback, findings from studies in the 1980s (Cohen & McKeachie, 1980; Menges & Brinko, 1986) to the present (Bell & Mladenovic, 2008; McShannon & Hynes, 2005) document the positive effects on teaching and student learning of peer observation coupled with feedback from a teaching consultant or knowledgeable peer.

At the same time, these approaches require a significant investment of time in terms of planning and implementation. They also require training of faculty and center staff in leadership, observation, and facilitation. Center directors with a small staff simply may not feel equipped to offer these more intensive development opportunities. They may also feel pressure to measure success by generating greater numbers of events rather than fewer activities of potentially higher impact. But in the attempt to reach many people, are center directors using their time and talents to the best effect? Can they step back and rethink ways to deliver services to faculty? In turn, we acknowledge that even an approach with the highest ranking is unlikely to be successful if it is not appropriate for the local context. What matters most and works best has to accommodate local needs, challenges, and circumstances.

Conclusion

The approaches that faculty developers use most to deliver services in their centers are 1- to 3-hour workshops, individual consultations, and Web-based resources. Each of these approaches is responsive to the hectic schedules of faculty members. Conversely, the approaches that directors are interested in expanding (e.g., FLCs, institutes, and peer observation) are ones in which their centers are currently less engaged, and they require new forms and levels of faculty time and involvement. These latter approaches, however, reflect what research suggests are particularly effective strategies for bringing about change in teaching skills, behaviors, and attitudes, as well as student learning. Thus, the process of exploring and adapting these new approaches offers an opportunity for innovation in faculty development work. The least-used approaches by centers are technology based, but there is some interest in adding asynchronous online programs, more Web-based resources, and webinars to the portfolio of approaches, should resources be available to do so. As center directors are challenged in the future to make the most of the time faculty spend together (as well as time spent with academic leaders, staff, and students), perhaps relationships can be deepened and efficiencies can be gained through the selective use of high-tech solutions to support high-touch approaches.

Chapter Highlights

- Across all institutional types, centers use workshops, individual consultations, and Web-based resources to the greatest extent. They are least likely to use approaches such as SGIDs, webinars, and asynchronous online programs.
- Centers use five approaches at a *slight to moderate* extent, including informal discussions, customized workshops for departments, seminars in a series, teaching observations and feedback with a consultant, and FLCs.
- Directors reported that the programs they consider to be signature for their centers closely track those programs they report that they offer the most, specifically hands-on workshops and individual consultations.
- Approaches that directors would like to expand if given the resources to do so include potentially more effective approaches such as FLCs, intensive institutes of two days or more, and peer observation of teaching with feedback.

6

WHERE ARE WE GOING?

One of the most important purposes of this study is to explore what faculty developers believe the future holds in store for them, their centers, and the field and what core assumptions they might need to rethink. Predicting the future is difficult in the best of times and the stablest of circumstances, and as the prior chapters demonstrate, the field of faculty development is in a dynamic era. Certainly, centers at all institutional types have continued over the past decade to focus on core services (including new faculty development, instructional technology, and evidence-based pedagogies). At the same time, many are reporting growth in new areas (e.g., course and curriculum reform) and a wish to extend their foci, for example, toward programming specifically for midcareer and senior faculty, support for SoTL, and high-engagement approaches (e.g., FLCs). This chapter looks back on what developers saw as future directions in 2006, examines how those predictions were borne out in 2016, and explores what developers see as the likely and hopeful scenarios for the field as it moves through the next decade to 2026 and beyond.

Developers' Predictions and Hopes in 2006

The responses from developers in Chapters 1 through 5 allow us to reflect on how predictive the 2006 respondents were in the areas they identified as likely, and as ideal, for those in the field to address. The next sections discuss the predictions made in 2006 and to what degree they were realized in 2016.

Developers' 2006 Predictions of Where the Field Would Go

In Sorcinelli, Austin, Eddy, and Beach (2006), the directions that developers thought the field would likely take were dominated by technology and assessment of student learning outcomes. Many of those developers expressed strong concerns about aspects of that scenario. They did not want faculty development relegated to technology assistance, nor did they want to see assessment narrowed to providing data for accountability rather than insight for the improvement of learning and teaching.

A decade later, technology is indeed central among the issues faculty developers reported as important to respond to on their campuses. Specifically, the integration of technology into traditional classrooms is among the top services developers reported addressing in their programs in the current study, at an extent equal to that reported in the earlier study. In addition, developers in the current study reported addressing online and blended learning to a moderate extent (this was a new item in the current study, reflecting a recognition of the advancement of these teaching technologies over the past decade). Directors in the current study also reported that they collaborate extensively with technology support units on their campuses (77% reporting such collaboration to a *moderate* or *great extent*), and that technology support units offer their own faculty development programming as well (67% of the respondents reporting such collaboration to a *moderate* or *great extent*; Table 2.3). The concern expressed in 2006 that the focus of faculty development would be dominated by technology and that centers for teaching and learning would be tasked with technology support was not surprising in a time of budget cuts and an increasing focus on efficiency in course delivery. Fortunately, however, current responses paint a more balanced picture of the place of technology support in centers' programming and the extent to which that support is shared with (or is the primary responsibility of) other units on campuses.

The assessment of student learning outcomes also remains among the most important services provided in recent years (reported in the current study at an extent equal to that reported in 2006). Responding to a new item in the current survey (added to reflect the growing demand for program-level as well as course-based assessment by institutions and accrediting agencies), developers indicated that they address program assessment to a *slight* to *moderate extent* (Table 4.1). In addition, center directors pointed out that support of faculty assessment of student learning outcomes is shared, at least to some extent, with assessment offices on campuses (Table 2.3). In fact, more than half (54%) of directors indicated that they collaborate with assessment offices to a *moderate* or *great extent*. However, it should be noted that some directors, particularly from liberal arts and community colleges, reported that they do not have such an office on campus to collaborate with. Further, assessment offices that do exist are not offering development and support services to the extent offered by technology offices. Eighty-three percent of directors reported that the assessment offices on their campuses offer faculty development programming *not at all* or to a *slight extent.*

Developers' 2006 Predictions of Where the Field Should Move

In 2006, in addition to identifying where they thought the field *would* move, developers identified five areas in which they thought the field *should* move: integrating technology into teaching and learning; deepening active pedagogies; addressing new and expanding roles of faculty and helping faculty balance those roles; building interdisciplinary communities of practice among faculty; and addressing issues of diversity for students, faculty, and institutions. Responses in the current study regarding services and approaches advanced by teaching and learning centers since 2006 offer a portrait of goals accomplished and goals not yet attained.

There is significant evidence in the current study that these five areas have been addressed. Integrating technology is among the top three signature programs mentioned in the current study; the University of South Dakota's program (described in Chapter 4) exemplifies the thoughtful approaches taken. It is difficult to measure precisely the full extent of center directors' efforts to effect such integration over the course of the past decade because these efforts have taken new forms such as hybrid and online course design. Having said that, it appears that pedagogical priorities have driven technology, and not the opposite (a theme we see developed more fully when we look forward to the next decade).

Deepening active, evidence-based pedagogies was a key area developers identified as important in 2006, and one that they felt the field should address moving forward. In the past decade, focus on this area has increased (as discussed in Chapter 4) and is among the top three signature services.

The importance to the field of addressing the new and expanding roles of faculty can be seen in the increase in orientation and development programs for part-time and fixed-term faculty, and in the interest in programs to support underserved, midcareer, and senior faculty. In addition, new faculty orientation is currently the top issue addressed by services and the top signature service. Directors' recognition that there is still significant work to be done to support faculty in all their roles can be seen in the areas they wish to expand: midcareer and senior career faculty support, leadership development, mentoring, and scholarly writing, among others. In sum, the hopeful, optimistic view of what the field should address has been realized in part but with a strong sense that more can and needs to be done.

The final two areas developers in 2006 indicated they believed the field should focus on in the coming decade—building interdisciplinary communities of faculty and addressing the complexities of diversity among students, faculty, and institutions—were reported in the current survey as being addressed *to a slight extent* in the form of FLCs, mentoring programs for underrepresented faculty, and diversity and multiculturalism related to teaching. Directors also saw a need for further progress in these areas and wished to expand related faculty development efforts.

Future Directions for Faculty Development—Near Term

We report here any result that has been identified by 15% or more of developers in any one of the institutional categories. This section looks at near-term imperatives. We asked a series of questions about the kinds of issues and approaches developers believed the field should focus on in the next five years. We presented the same 39 items in Chapters 4 and 5 pertaining to issues for which they offered services and approaches they used for delivering programs. We asked developers to identify the top three issues and the top three approaches faculty development should focus on over the next five years. In this way, we had direct, comparable data to responses about signature services, services to expand, issues to address, and approaches to faculty development. The percentages we present represent the extent to which developers identified an item among their top three.

Top Issues to Address in the Next Five Years

When considering the issues the field should prioritize, responses focused heavily on the instructional dimension. Table 6.1 contains the top responses to the question of what issues or services the field should focus on in the next five years. Assessment of student learning outcomes was chosen by the largest percentage of respondents, with high support from those in research and doctoral (21%) and comprehensive (25%) universities. Teaching in online and distance environments was also selected as a strong priority (16%), but much more so in research and doctoral universities (21%) than in the other types of institutions. Multiculturalism and diversity related to teaching (13%) and course and curriculum reform (12%) are among the top choices, driven by the priority community colleges give them (23% for each). Although developers see instructional issues at the forefront of their near-term priorities, they also seem aware that they may need to focus on broader institutional issues. We encourage readers to explore these issues in their own institutional types (listed in Appendix C).

TABLE 6.1

**Issues Faculty Development Should Address in the Next Five Years
by Institutional Type**

Issues	Percentage of Directors					
	All	*R/D*	*Comp*	*LA*	*CC*	*Can*
Assessment of student learning outcomes (T&L)	18%	21%	25%	13%	17%	9%
Teaching in online and distance environments (T&L)	16%	21%	10%	13%	9%	12%
Multiculturalism and diversity related to teaching (T&L)	13%	12%	9%	16%	23%	15%
Course and curriculum reform (EII)	12%	9%	19%	11%	23%	3%

Note. N = 385; unreported = 0. T&L = teaching and learning; EII = educational and institutional improvement; R/D = research/doctoral institutions; Comp = comprehensive institutions; LA = liberal arts colleges; CC = community colleges; Can = Canadian institutions.

Top Approaches to Focus On in the Next Five Years

Developers were also asked about the top three approaches (out of a possible set of 15) that faculty development should emphasize in the next five years. Highlights of the results appear in Table 6.2, and the complete set of responses is in Appendix C. The approaches developers thought faculty development should focus on differed somewhat from the approaches they most wanted to add or expand in their own centers (discussed in Chapter 5). FLCs top the list with 36% of developers identifying this as an approach the field should focus on, and by a wide margin in U.S. institutions, as when directors reported which approaches they would like to add or expand (43%; Table 5.3). Beyond their interest in FLCs, directors by institutional type are more diverse in their other responses. Developers from all institutional types were more attracted to technology-driven approaches as a focus for the field than directors were when they reported approaches to expand in their own centers. Asynchronous online programs, webinars, and Web-based resources all garnered significant interest across most institutional types (with the exception of community colleges). Apparently, developers are more interested in the field as a whole, taking the lead on creating a more flexible, time-efficient set of delivery and engagement approaches, than they are in adding such approaches to the work of their centers.

TABLE 6.2

Approaches Faculty Development Should Address In the Next Five Years by Institutional Type

Approaches	Percentage of Directors					
	All	*R/D*	*Comp*	*LA*	*CC*	*Can*
Faculty and professional learning communities (i.e., full semester or academic year, regular meetings)	36%	36%	41%	40%	43%	27%
Asynchronous online programs	19%	20%	16%	29%	6%	14%
Web-based resources (e.g., links to articles or Internet content)	18%	17%	29%	16%	6%	18%
Webinars (1- to 2- hour synchronous Web-based seminars that can be saved and viewed later)	17%	17%	17%	26%	11%	18%
Institutes/retreats (2–3 full days)	16%	17%	20%	16%	14%	3%
Department/discipline-specific workshops (on demand)	16%	14%	20%	16%	31%	15%
Peer observation of teaching with feedback	13%	13%	17%	13%	14%	6%
Individual consultation	12%	15%	15%	11%	9%	6%
Seminars (multiple-meeting commitment)	8%	8%	9%	5%	17%	3%

Note. N = 263; unreported = 122. R/D = research/doctoral institutions; Comp = comprehensive institutions; LA = liberal arts colleges; CC = community colleges; Can = Canadian institutions.

Developers at liberal arts institutions, somewhat surprisingly, showed the greatest interest in the field's addressing asynchronous online faculty development programs (29%) and offering webinars (26%), perhaps because such centers often operate with minimal staff. Comprehensive institution developers indicated Web-based resources as an approach to emphasize (29%) to a greater extent than other institutions, perhaps for the same reason, although they also indicated that intensive institutes and department-based programming are important (20% each). Technology-driven approaches were not the top priority for community colleges. Rather, these directors were more interested in seeing the field address department- and discipline-specific programs (31%), seminars, and other face-to-face approaches. They also identified FLCs as a priority for the field (43%) to a greater degree than did developers at other institutional types, although there was considerable interest in FLCs across institutional types. Taken together, the data suggest that developers perceive that faculty development as a field should emphasize the long-term opportunities and deep engagement that FLCs provide. At the same time, however, they see a need for harnessing the potential of the Internet to serve their stakeholders and want the field to focus on approaches that reach beyond the bounds of synchronous, face-to-face programming.

Directions for Faculty Development in the Next Decade: Open-Ended Responses

The final set of questions in both the 2006 and 2016 studies asked faculty developers to reflect on and respond to the following open-ended questions: (a) Which directions do you think the field of faculty development will take in the next decade? and (b) In which directions do you think the field should move? We invited respondents to write anything they wished in any length they deemed necessary. More than two thirds of respondents to the current study commented on these two questions, providing a rich set of thoughtful responses. We analyzed responses with the same coding scheme used in the prior study, with additions of new codes when necessary to capture ideas that were new to this group of respondents. Themes that emerged from that qualitative content analysis are presented as well as quotes that help give context and voice to the responses. Developers' predictions of what directions the field should and will move in the next decade continue many of the themes delineated in our 2006 study while also breaking some new ground.

Two issues appear overwhelmingly in responses regarding where faculty development as a field *will* move and where it *should* move: assessment of student learning and online, distance, and blended learning. Two additional responses regarding where the field *will* go involve technology, including technology integration into traditional classrooms and Web-based, self-directed faculty development. Developers did not focus on these two issues quite as much when considering what directions faculty development *should* take in the next decade. Because there is significant overlap in the issues addressed through responses to these two open-ended questions, we discuss key areas of interest, contrast their importance, and offer a selection of comments from developers, organized by topic.

Developers' Comments on the Future of Faculty Development

Overall, assessment tops the 2016 list of directions in which faculty developers believe the field *should* move, and it is third on the list of directions in which they believe the field *will* move. Because of its importance in the national landscape with higher education, assessment as a broader theme of this entire study is discussed in depth in Chapter 7. Other areas that developers agreed the field should address include technology (especially online, blended, and distance learning), building interdisciplinary efforts and faculty communities, and SoTL and related approaches to critically reflective teaching.

Assessment

The comments of developers revealed their interest in assessment of both student learning outcomes and the faculty development programs they offer. Their comments reflect the complex reactions they have to the growing emphasis on assessment across the higher education sector.

Assessment of Student Learning

Developers discussed extensively the opportunities and the potential limitations of the increased focus on assessment, evidence-based practice, and accreditation. In particular, they see helping faculty understand course design and program assessment processes as a way to also help them adopt more student-centered and active learning approaches. On the other hand, they see a danger in having *assessment* defined too narrowly on demonstration of student learning outcomes and using it for accountability, restricting the role of developers to that of assessment cops. These tensions were apparent in the comments of the 2006 developers and persist in the comments of developers in the current study.

> We are also seeing a greater interest in data that can inform discussions of course/curriculum revision, and I think we need to be able to help faculty think through, collect, and analyze such data while also making sure we have good data about the impact of our own services. (Research/doctoral, program coordinator)

> I fear that federal policy and "performance indicators" will suck the joy out of this work to the extent that we will become an extension of the measuring arm, being forced to report on what's easy to count instead of what's important to value. (Research/doctoral, faculty member)

> I think without strong leadership that provides a compelling vision of higher education as something more than a means to economic success, faculty

development will be drawn further toward supporting the assessment and commodification of knowledge and learners. (Research/doctoral, director)

We need to take on more leadership roles in student learning outcomes assessment (not conducting the assessment, but in helping academic units to design, implement, and think about assessment). (Research/doctoral, faculty member)

Assessment of Programs

Assessment beyond that of student learning was much more prominent in developers' comments in the current study compared to those in 2006. Developers are quite aware of the need to support academic program assessment as well as the need to assess their own programs. Several noted that they are being asked by those to whom they report to provide impact data on their programs. That kind of assessment was identified by directors as an area they need to develop.

Faculty development should move toward a more evidence-based approach where our practices are informed by the impact/outcome of our work. Additionally, evaluation needs to emanate from an intrinsic desire to gather evidence/feedback opposed to a focus on accountability. (Community college, director)

We will be asked for increasing support for assessment. I just hope we are given the power to approach it in instructionally meaningful ways, not just mechanical ones. We will also be called on to develop more partnerships with other units across campus as a way of better leveraging limited resources. (Community college, program coordinator)

Increasingly move toward program-level curriculum development support (including the assessment of program learning outcomes)—which also leads to just-in-time faculty development with all members of academic units (not just those who would otherwise come to the Centre). (Community college, director).

The accountability under which K–12 teachers have operated for the past 20 years is coming to higher education, and we are not ready. Accreditation processes now speak about student outcomes, but working with faculty to understand how that accountability will affect their teaching is still novel. (Community college, associate/assistant director)

The field should become more evidence-based, both in what we (as faculty developers) do and in what we offer to our faculty colleagues. The field should become more closely aligned with the needs of academic departments and disciplines. (Community college, instructional consultant/designer/coordinator)

Technology

Beyond the issue of assessment, directions in which our 2016 respondents believed the field would and should move continued to be dominated by technology, as it had been in the previous study. Important directions included online, blended, and distance learning; technology integration in the classroom; and Web-based and self-directed faculty development. The technology noted in future directions reflects the significant expansion of Web-based platforms and tools, and their facilitation of new kinds of course delivery. Online, hybrid, and blended courses have expanded greatly and are becoming the norm in many institutions. Developers seem more sanguine about their role in supporting integration of technology into the classroom than they were in 2006 and more pragmatic about the need to focus on online, blended, and hybrid teaching and learning as a key area for programming. In 2006 we saw deep concern and not much celebration of the potential of technology to transform teaching and learning, but in 2016 we see many more developers acknowledging and excited about the opportunities technology offers for reaching students and reshaping higher education more generally. Developers seem to be embracing the idea that the field can and should provide leadership in promoting best practices for technology-enhanced teaching and learning in all its forms. Developers also recognize the potential for a rise in Web-based and self-directed faculty development, although they are not unanimous in their support of it. Particularly as the number of part-time and distance instructors increases, technology-supported faculty development opportunities may help universities and colleges serve their needs.

Online, Blended, and Distance Learning

I think the field needs to find ways to engage faculty who have increasingly busy lives and who need help keeping up with the latest technologies. In addition, faculty seem to be taken with the idea of flipped classrooms, which may be exactly the lever that will lead to a more widespread adaptation of active learning methods. (Research/doctoral, program coordinator)

Stop viewing online education as a threat, and advocate for how online education, when done correctly, can be a powerful learning environment. (Canadian institution, director)

Use of technology in creating interactive learning environments, whether online, f2f [face-to-face], or blended [coupled with a] deep understanding of pedagogy and its implementation in various contexts (traditional undergrads, adult learners, online courses). (Research/doctoral, program coordinator)

Technology in the Classroom

I believe we need to continue to expand our offerings to support faculty as they strive to combine traditional teaching methods and approaches with the vast resources available online and in technology. (Comprehensive, director)

I think it must move toward greater uses of technology, but I hope that's in the directions I described—[in other words] using technology tools and online information to support more personal, collaborative learning experiences for faculty. (Research/doctoral, senior-level administrator)

Totally embrace instructional technology so that it becomes invisible, just another tool to support good instructional design, effective teaching and student access, engagement and learning. Should hire more instructional designers and instructional technologist[s] as part of the team. Determine when and what types of technology are appropriate in any learning situation. (Canadian institution, director)

Web-Based, Self-Directed Faculty Development

Need to move away from total reliance on on-campus, face-to-face workshops for everything and start using a blended approach using online education effectively to meet the needs of busy faculty and geographically dispersed faculty. (Canadian institution, director)

Online/hybrid development will increasingly dominate. Doing faculty development without a substantial technology component will become difficult or impossible in many areas within the next 10 years—I would argue we are there already if you're talking about what we should be doing as opposed to what we are doing. (Other type of institution, director)

At a community college where 50% of our courses are being taught by adjuncts, I believe distance faculty development and Web-based faculty development have to happen sooner than later. (Research/doctoral, assistant/associate director)

There appears to be more reliance on Web-based learning and not enough opportunities for social and transformative learning about the practice of teaching. (Comprehensive, director)

Online resources and webinars. Time is such an issue that faculty won't commit to seminars and meetings. (Community college, senior-level administrator)

I think there will be more focus on technology. As a faculty developer, I think this is necessary, but often frustrating because the tools and resources change so rapidly. I have never attended a session or conference on teaching with technology where I walked away feeling confident in my ability to use or teach about whatever tools were being presented. (Research/doctoral, instructional consultant/designer/coordinator)

Interdisciplinary Communities

The walls among disciplines are lowering. Faculty developers see an increased need for interdisciplinarity in addressing complex issues and problems that have implications for curricular development, teaching, and faculty research. Their ambiguity and mixed analyses are reflected in their comments.

Added emphasis on reengagement of the more experienced faculty for mentoring and training of the newer faculty. Added focus on cross-discipline networking and collaboration. (Liberal arts, faculty member)

Emphasis on collaborative learning about teaching and learning. More cross-disciplinary discussion and interaction to improve the comprehensive knowledge of curriculum and the impact of teaching strategies. (Comprehensive, senior-level administrator)

Faculty need to be working with each other in an interdisciplinary fashion in peer review, seminars, and communities of practice. We need cross-fertilization of ideas, not the siloing that is so prominent. (Community college, senior-level administrator)

SoTL and Reflective Teaching

At the same time that they see technology increasing as a focus of their work and a means by which they can reach those they serve, developers are not willing to give up on the powerful approaches that build and sustain communities of practice among faculty. Indeed, they want to invest more in highly relational approaches that support faculty engagement with ideas of teaching and learning as scholarly work. The rise in interest in SoTL and the identification of reflective practice and interdisciplinary communities as priorities for the next decade indicate strong interest among developers for deeper involvement with and for faculty across disciplines.

> More just-in-time, very personal engagement of faculty with one another around topics of professional and instructional development, through professional learning communities, mentorships, peer evaluation. All should be grounded in SoTL methods, or at least in evidence-based approaches. (Research/doctoral, senior-level administrator)

> Faculty development as a field should work to increase collaboration across disciplines—on SoTL research as well as development of shared knowledge of best practices in teaching. (Comprehensive, director)

> I think the field of faculty development SHOULD build communities of faculty that work together to address issues in higher education. One-shot workshops should become a thing of the past—rather, working groups should really delve into hot topics or issues and do some real work (course redesign, SoTL study design, etc.). (Other type of institution, senior-level administrator)

> In the next decade faculty development should focus on the implementation of the scholarship of teaching and learning into practice. We already have a very clear concept of what defines *good teaching*. We need to establish an environment where good teaching is valued and rewarded in the same way and regarded at the same level as excellence in research. (Comprehensive, faculty member; emphasis added)

> We think there is great need to fulfill Lee Shulman's idea that teaching needs to be public property: we need to help faculty become more comfortable with greater transparency and openness about what they do, what their students do and say about it, how others see what they do. And we need to help faculty value this transparency more. (Comprehensive, faculty member)

Other Views of the Future of the Field

In addition to highlighting themes developers mentioned most frequently as important future directions for the field, we include their comments on three emergent themes with potential impacts: faculty development in the disciplines, an increasing focus on institutional change, and the financing of faculty development. We end this section with comments that reaffirm developers' commitment to the traditional focus of faculty development on the needs of the faculty. Taken together, the themes and comments presented previously and in this section capture the collective wisdom of developers as they reflect on the future of faculty development as a field.

Faculty Development in the Disciplines

The more development/training content goes online, the less the need for a dedicated teaching and learning center. Instead, colleges and large departments will have dedicated positions with access to locally created and nationally published training resources. An administrative position might be used to coordinate all these positions but will likely be more within the college level. (Liberal arts, faculty member)

Another thing that will change is the approach to support for teaching and learning. The culture of the academy is what's/who's down the hall. Support for teaching and learning will be more discipline specific with teaching consultants and instructional designers working in a distributed model with support in the departments. (Comprehensive, faculty member)

The field should become more closely aligned with the needs of academic departments and disciplines. (Community college, instructional consultant/designer/coordinator)

I think our offerings will be more tailored to the needs of faculty (not one size fits all, but programming directed to health sciences instructors, for instance). (Liberal arts, director)

[There is] a blurring of boundaries between centers and other units and players interested in student learning and faculty development. Hard to know if centers will even look like they look now in 10 years—maybe standing alone and stronger, maybe merged, maybe closed depending on campus context. (Research/doctoral, senior-level administrator)

Institutional/Organizational Development

Becoming a core institutional resource for the promotion and development of effective teaching and learning; act as institutional change agents; be resources at the table for key educational debates. (Research/doctoral, director)

Educational reform efforts, with larger multi-institutional grants; organizational change and organizational development. (Institutional type not provided, senior-level administrator)

Focus on large institutional issues (changes in institutional culture related to assessment, use of technology). (Comprehensive, senior-level administrator)

Greater ability to address individual and cohort-based faculty professional development needs while aligning programs toward strategic or other institutional needs. Drawing on expertise in faculty development to provide greater advising and input on, and support of, institutional issues such as learning outcomes assessment, faculty evaluation, faculty recruitment and hiring, student retention, and online curriculum and teaching. (Community college, senior-level administrator)

Faculty development has become everyone's business with foundations, federal government, professional associations, and even schools and colleges now establishing their own centers or associate deans for faculty development. It is increasingly difficult to read the tea leaves and plan in a thoughtful and strategic way. Clearly expertise in organizational/systems development will be helpful as we go forward. But mechanisms for continually assessing the pulse of the faculty will also be important—equally important.

Due to resource constraints, faculty development needs to become more strategic in aligning its work with the needs of faculty and academic units. (Community college, director)

Programs and systems/tools that are integrated with other campus units, procedures, groups, and systems. In other words, faculty development that is part of the normal procedures, functions, and systems that are used and followed by campus departments, colleges, and administrators. (Research/doctoral, director)

The field needs to move toward stronger support of the key university educational priorities established by university leaders. (Research/doctoral, director)

Toward organizational development, rather than focusing so specifically on how to enact relatively minor elements of the faculty role. Toward a greater understanding of and mindful use of communications technology. (Liberal arts, director)

I think it will resist shifting from largely an instructional development mode—it is too enamored with helping and the immediate rewards of that work; it is too focused on individual development and will reluctantly reposition itself to conceive of its work at an institutional level. I think we have the potential to become significant and highly valued experts and partners, or shift into less visible and easily reduced services. (Research/doctoral, director)

We'll tackle that challenge, but probably through the lens of leadership development or organizational development. I worry that faculty and administrators won't understand what we're doing if we talk about those lenses publicly, however. We'll also continue to focus a lot of energy on individual faculty and courses. That's important work, but it won't help address the more global challenges to higher education. (Research/doctoral, director)

Funding for Faculty Development/Financial Constraints

Fewer resources mean that fewer interactions will be built over common food, space, and community. Faculty development efforts will likely be pressed yet further to make something out of nothing—and it is hard to build community without a hook—no matter HOW GOOD the offerings!! (Research/doctoral, director)

Judging from my institutional context, financial resources and the lack thereof will drive the development. Our center will need to become even more self-sustaining and find new revenue streams (grants and tuition for programs, etc.). (Research/doctoral, senior-level administrator)

Given tight budgets, I'm concerned that faculty development will become a lower priority for administrators and that they will look to cheap fixes that reduce personalized support for faculty development. While Internet resources are valuable, and asynchronous workshops are certainly an important tool, they are not a substitute for personalized means of faculty development through mentoring, coaching, and workshops that address specific areas of need. (Liberal arts, senior-level administrator)

If funding continues to decline (as it has in California and many other states), it is possible that faculty development (and professional development for all staff in higher education) will be wiped out! The only thing that could save professional development is strict accreditation requirements to show how professional development fits into the overall institutional mission, planning, and efforts to increase student success. (Research/doctoral, director)

My fear is that with shrinking budgets things like teaching and learning centers and funding could get cut. This is wrong, but budgets are tight and sometimes it seems that development can be cut. In the short term this seems appropriate but the long term will be bad. I think adding assessment and accreditation to development is pedagogically sound, and I think it will help centers and funding for development survive. (Research/doctoral, senior-level administrator)

Responding to the Needs of Faculty

Faculty development at any institution should be driven by the desires of the faculty, supported by the administration, and have the necessary resources to carry out the plan. Actively including the diversity of voices and opinions in this process in the next decade would be useful. (Research/doctoral, senior-level administrator)

We have to see how higher education evolves in our own contexts and be prepared to offer whatever support is needed. If there is a push from the faculty for ePortfolios, for example, then we need to be ready to create the support that will be needed both for the faculty and the institution. (Comprehensive, director)

I think faculty development needs to be more available to the variation of faculty needs. Some faculty prefer face-to-face workshops and others need online resources just-in-time. We need to be flexible in our offerings to meet these various types of needs, by offering a variety of modes. (Liberal arts, faculty member)

I think that faculty development should maintain emphasis on relationship-based consulting and a human touch. (Liberal arts, faculty member)

More than ever faculty developers serve as occupational counselors that help faculty members construct a professional identity. Faculty developers have the unique opportunity to help faculty find role clarity, social acceptance, and self-efficacy as an educator in a changing profession. (Research/doctoral, director)

I do see a continued need for one-on-one and small group connections—consultation and learning communities. Faculty are so busy and the pace of life has changed so much from the early days of faculty development that I worry that the interpersonal connections and conversations about learning, teaching, and faculty life will be a challenge to sustain and centers will have to be more creative in figuring out how to do so. (Canadian institution, senior-level administrator)

Chapter Highlights

- In 2006 respondents thought faculty development would move strongly in the directions of technology integration into teaching and learning, and assessment. The current study supports those predictions.
- In 2006 respondents thought faculty development as a field should move toward greater emphasis on meaningfully integrating technology into teaching and learning; deepening active pedagogies; addressing new and expanding roles of faculty and helping faculty balance those roles; building interdisciplinary communities of practice among faculty; and addressing issues of diversity for students, faculty, and institutions. The current study indicates growth in some areas and a recognition of the need for further work in others.
- Near-term service priorities for attention by the field are strongly focused on teaching and learning: online and distance learning, active and inquiry-based learning, integration of technology into traditional classrooms, and assessment of student learning. FLCs are considered the program approach the field should embrace most in the next five years.
- Long-term directions for the field continue to focus on technology in several forms and assessment of student learning and programs. Developers also believe the field should move toward greater emphasis on SoTL, organizational development, and individual consultation and the needs of individual faculty. However, they believe those in the field will need to address issues of tight funding and the need for alternative financing streams to stay viable in an increasingly strained higher education context. They note the rise in, and the need to continue thinking about, faculty development that is discipline based or arising from the disciplines, and they see their role in institutional change necessarily increasing.

7

HOW DOES ASSESSMENT FIT
IN OUR WORK?

Assessment, in multiple forms and for multiple purposes, has been a topic of growing importance in higher education research and faculty development for many years (Chism & Szabo, 1998; Hutchings, 2010; Wehlburg, 2010). A precise definition of the term *assessment* can be difficult to parse because it is applied to activities such as student learning outcomes, academic program review, performance benchmarking, and quality measurement, each of which has numerous manifestations in academic environments (Welsh & Metcalf, 2003). In fact, higher education has experienced a tension between activities such as performance benchmarking and student learning outcomes assessment for decades. This tension is sometimes identified as the difference between assessment for accountability—seemingly an administrative concern—and assessment for improvement—seemingly a faculty concern (Ewell, 2009; Sorcinelli & Garner, 2013).

These tensions have been at work in the field of faculty development for some time as well. In our earlier study, developers identified assessment of student learning outcomes as one of the top three challenges facing faculty and institutions, and they believed this challenge could and should be addressed through faculty development. Developers at the time placed high importance on providing services related to assessing student learning (mean = 3.43) but rated their centers' capacity to offer such services much more modestly (mean = 2.57) (Sorcinelli, Austin, Eddy, & Beach 2006). Although developers embraced classroom-based assessment and research, in which faculty engage in reflection and inquiry about their teaching practices and student learning, many worried about the potential pressures to be part of various accountability systems their institutions found "important for business purposes rather than educational ones" (p. 136). Others argued that if faculty development moved more deliberately into the broader arena of outcomes assessment, and administrators of institutions recognized developers' expertise in this area, faculty development would be seen as essential for individual faculty members' growth and for institutional quality.

In the introduction to this book, we laid out the internal and external forces driving the increased attention to issues of assessment and accountability in higher education over the past decade. We introduced the idea that the field of faculty development may be entering an Age of Evidence, characterized by a focus on evidence-based teaching and learning, interest in research on teaching practices in the disciplines (discipline-based education research), assessment of student learning outcomes, and institutional needs for quality improvement. Throughout this book, data have shown that assessment is an important service focus, a fruitful area for collaboration, and a strong future direction. In this chapter, we further our case for the emergence of the Age of Evidence by considering the ways faculty developers think about and engage with assessment in their work. We first present new findings on the methods faculty developers use to assess the impact of their programs. We then turn to an analysis of the qualitative open-ended data and discuss findings regarding developers' views of three kinds of assessment: assessment of teaching and learning processes and outcomes, assessment of faculty work as instructors, and assessment of academic program outcomes connected with institutional improvement and accreditation. Throughout the discussion, we interweave a selection of developers' open-ended comments and reflections on this often-mentioned topic.

How Faculty Development Directors Assess Their Programs

Almost two decades ago, Chism and Szabo (1998) found that faculty developers were assessing their programs in encouraging numbers but using fairly superficial measures to do so. Hines (2009) documented the same situation through interviews with developers. She noted that although there was a significant lack of systematic assessment of programs among her study participants, there was an equally significant interest in assessment.

That interest guided our decision to include a section of new questions in our current survey, probing ways that faculty developers assess the quality and impact of the programs they offer and how they disseminate the results of that assessment. On the survey, directors were asked to rate the extent to which they collected data on key faculty development outcomes, the methods they used in that collection, and the kinds of dissemination they used to share the results of their assessments. Table 7.1 presents the outcomes directors report measuring, including numbers of community members served, satisfaction with a program, self-reported increase in skills, and changes in student learning or institutional practices.

TABLE 7.1

Extent to Which Directors Report Data Collected on Faculty Development Outcomes

Outcomes	All M (SD)	R/D M (SD)	Comp M (SD)	LA M (SD)	CC M (SD)	Can M (SD)
N	160	70	38	13	16	15
Numbers served through your programs	3.78 (0.52)	3.72 (0.54)	3.92 (0.36)	3.92 (0.28)	3.69 (0.79)	3.67 (0.49)
Satisfaction of participants	3.53 (0.69)	3.50 (0.68)	3.58 (0.68)	3.69 (0.63)	3.50 (0.89)	3.53 (0.52)
Increase in the knowledge or skills of the participants	2.70 (0.92)	2.84 (0.89)	2.82 (0.87)	2.23 (0.93)	2.56 (1.15)	2.53 (0.92)
Change in the practice of participants	2.54 (0.90)	2.69 (0.86)	2.51 (0.93)	2.31 (0.95)	2.38 (1.03)	2.33 (0.98)
Change in the learning or behavior of those served by the participants	2.15 (0.94)	2.31 (0.96)	2.20 (0.83)	1.54 (0.66)	2.21 (1.05)	2.07 (1.14)
Change in the institution	2.07 (0.94)	2.12 (0.96)	2.14 (0.96)	2.00 (0.91)	2.19 (1.05)	1.77 (0.83)
Other data gathered	2.59 (1.37)	2.63 (1.41)	2.17 (1.47)	2.00 (—)	4.00 (—)	4.00 (—)

Note. N = 161; unreported = 32. 1 = not at all; 2 = to a slight extent; 3 = to a moderate extent; 4 = to a great extent. R/D = research/doctoral institutions; Comp = comprehensive institutions; LA = liberal arts colleges; CC = community colleges; Can = Canadian institutions. Dashes indicate no data reported.

The program outcomes measured to the greatest extent include participation numbers and participant satisfaction. All institutions collect data for these outcomes at equal levels, which is no surprise, given that attendance and satisfaction are easiest to measure and tend to be standard metrics expected of and reported by many faculty development programs. Data on increases in the knowledge or skill and change in practice of participants are collected, on average, between a *slight* and *moderate extent* and tend to be self-reported changes that can also be collected in a straightforward manner. Research and comprehensive universities address these outcomes to a slightly greater extent than the other types of institutions. Measuring changes in learning or behavior of students is exponentially more difficult to accomplish, as exemplified in the responses. No directors reported doing so more than *to a slight extent.*

Measuring changes in the institution requires for measurable goals set at that level to depend on specific programming. Given those difficulties, it is admirable that some directors are reporting such assessment even *to a slight extent*. At the student and institutional level, directors may be relying more on anecdote or informal data to determine impact.

Data Collection Methods for Assessment

We next asked directors to identify the kinds of data they collect to assess the key program outcomes they identified. They were able to choose as many methods for each outcome as they wished. The percentages reported in Table 7.2 represent the percentage of directors who chose a particular method for a particular outcome.

Overall, the kinds of methods directors use to collect data are well aligned with the key outcomes measured. For example, self-report surveys are useful for satisfaction and can support assessment of participants' increases in knowledge. Likewise, planned research projects are necessary to fully assess changes in teaching practice and their connection to changes in student learning. Although centers are tracking their numbers and gathering self-report data from their participants, they are not employing the kind of assessment practices they are likely recommending in their workshops and other programming. Observation of teaching, collection of examples of student work (or syllabi and other artifacts of instructional change) that demonstrate achievement of learning outcomes, and planned data collection, such as is done in SoTL, are being used by only a handful of directors. Admittedly, it is far more difficult to collect follow-up data from faculty than it is for faculty members to collect assessment data from students in their courses. And linking faculty development programming in any measurable way to improved student learning requires knowledge and skills, time, and resources that the average faculty development center does not have (Hines, 2009). These results were reinforced by interviews with directors about their signature programs. They reported collecting data on participation and satisfaction, but few reported building pre- and postexperience assessments into their programs, following up with participants with impact surveys or interviews, or observing participants. Many indicated that they knew they needed to do so but just did not have the time or resources to accomplish that level or depth of assessment.

Dissemination of Assessment Results

We asked directors how they disseminate the results of their own program assessments to determine how widely they distribute communications regarding their center's activities. We offered a list of five common methods of

TABLE 7.2
Data Collection Methods for Assessment of Key Outcomes

Data Collection Methods	Numbers Served Through Programs	Satisfaction of Participants	Increase in Knowledge or Skills of Participants	Change in the Practice of Participants	Change in Student Learning or Behavior	Change in the Institution
Participation tracking and record collection	78%	19%	14%	12%	6%	10%
Participant self-report surveys	20%	73%	56%	47%	28%	20%
Interviews	4%	22%	21%	25%	12%	14%
Observation	11%	11%	24%	28%	11%	26%
Collection of student assignments, projects, exam scores	1%	2%	5%	5%	10%	6%
Planned research projects that assess change	4%	5%	17%	19%	19%	20%
Tracking of development and dissemination of SoTL projects by faculty	8%	3%	13%	15%	11%	11%

Note. N = 162; unreported = 31. SoTL = scholarship of teaching and learning.

dissemination and the option to choose and describe other methods. Directors could choose multiple outlets to best represent their practices. Table 7.3 presents the percentage of methods reported by institutional type. There was a surprisingly even spread across the methods directors used. Fewer than 20% of all institutions indicated they did not disseminate results at all or skipped the question. Comprehensive universities were substantially more likely to use at least two reporting outlets and also were more likely to report three or more outlets.

TABLE 7.3
Number of Dissemination Methods Reported by Institutional Classification

Number of Methods	All	R/D	Comp	LA	CC	Can
0	18%	19%	9%	28%	6%	12%
1	20%	22%	12%	17%	41%	29%
2	29%	24%	40%	28%	29%	24%
3	16%	18%	21%	11%	6%	18%
4	12%	14%	12%	6%	12%	12%
5	5%	4%	7%	11%	6%	6%

Note. R/D = research/doctoral institutions; Comp = comprehensive institutions; LA = liberal arts colleges; CC = community colleges; Can = Canadian institutions.

TABLE 7.4
Methods Used to Disseminate the Results of Impact Assessments

	All	R/D	Comp	LA	CC	Can
Publication in an annual report	54%	52%	61%	61%	47%	65%
Report to an advisory board	50%	52%	54%	33%	53%	59%
Presentation at conferences or meetings external to one's campus	39%	39%	44%	39%	24%	47%
Presentation of data on the institution's website	23%	22%	33%	17%	18%	18%
Publication in journals, book chapters, or other broadly disseminated works	23%	22%	30%	22%	24%	12%
Other dissemination approaches	12%	9%	14%	11%	29%	6%

Note. N = 159; unreported = 34. R/D = research/doctoral institutions; Comp = comprehensive institutions; LA = liberal arts colleges; CC = community colleges; Can = Canadian institutions.

Across all institutional types, dissemination of assessment results takes place primarily through the publication of annual reports and reports to advisory boards (Table 7.4). There is some indication that directors are presenting assessment results at conferences, and there is some evidence for publication in scholarly outlets. Among the other responses were newsletters, reports to academic leadership, and presentations to faculty senates and other internal stakeholders.

Interesting institutional differences are apparent in the kinds of dissemination centers undertake. Overall, comprehensive universities and Canadian institutions appear to be most committed to disseminating their assessment results. Both report more presentations at external conferences, and comprehensive university directors report much higher rates of publication on university websites and in scholarly publications than any other institutional type. This dissemination pattern is very consistent with the undergraduate focus of comprehensive universities and their emphasis on teaching and learning. Directors of those centers may feel that such presentations and publications are more rewarded than might directors at research and doctoral institutions. The resources needed to support travel to present at conferences and the time to develop publications may be far scarcer at liberal arts and community colleges, as indicated in Chapter 3. This may limit the ability of directors in those institutions to disseminate their programs' results beyond the institution. Community colleges are far less likely to publish an annual report than comprehensive, liberal arts, or Canadian institutions, again perhaps reflecting resource scarcity. Liberal arts institutions may not have advisory board structures, accounting for their lower percentage for that particular method.

These findings align with those of prior research (e.g., Chism & Szabo, 1998; Hines, 2009) and indicate that assessment of their own programs is still a challenge for directors of centers that are underresourced and focused on meeting faculty needs as they arise. In a study of 15 years' worth of published faculty development assessment reports, Kuscera and Sviniki (2010) found only 10 that met criteria set by the federal government for "scientifically valid educational evaluation" (p. 6). This may not be as surprising as the numbers first indicate; such criteria include randomized controlled designs and other research approaches very difficult (and ethically challenging) to implement in professional development situations. The barriers to such evaluation include the complex and longitudinal nature of change; for example, an experienced faculty member is not likely to display statistically measurable change in short time frames or controlled environments. Kuscera and Sviniki joined with others in the field, in particular, Chism and Banta (2007), to advocate for a broadened definition of *rigor in evaluation* to guide faculty developers' assessment of the impacts of their programs. For example, Hurney, Harris, Prins, and Kruck's (2014) report that measured changes in learning or behavior of students based on learner self-reflection questions added to a midsemester evaluation is a strong example of the kind of assessment that is informative to the field and demonstrates impact but is relatively simple to integrate into an assessment plan.

Very recently, Condon, Iverson, Manduca, Rutz, and Willett (2016) reported the result of longitudinal, multimethod assessments of the impact of faculty development initiatives on faculty instructional practices, and, in turn, on student learning outcomes. They demonstrated clear connections from engagement in teaching enhancement workshops, learning communities, and other development approaches to long-term change in instructional practices. The faculty participants of these studies were also able to demonstrate lasting improvements in their students' learning. However, this rigorous and far-reaching assessment of faculty development impact is beyond the scope of the average center. The value it offers to faculty developers is that the interventions assessed as being effective are some of the most commonly used in faculty development: workshop series, consultations, and observations. Chism and Banta (2007) argue that individual faculty developers cannot and should not need to undertake similarly complex assessments but should be able to refer to those that already exist as evidence for the efficacy of programs they offer.

Faculty developers cannot and should not need to become educational researchers to demonstrate the worth of their programs. Because the research on the impact of effective teaching practices on student motivation and achievement is strong and consistent, there is no reason faculty developers would need to repeat that research. Demonstrating more clearly that the programming offered helps instructors adopt and adapt best practices is more important and more achievable. Fink (2013) discussed how starting with such assumptions of achievable demonstration can guide assessment and offered a set of innovative assessment approaches with examples from the literature. Developers can also use their networks to access the resources they do not have as a means to demonstrate impact. Assessment fellows, either faculty or staff, can undertake special projects that center staff do not have time for. Doctoral students in higher education, evaluation, or organizational psychology programs often need field experiences as part of their development. Likewise, graduate-level courses that involve program assessment and evaluation often seek cases students can use to apply the concepts and tools they are acquiring. Developers also can consult with other units on campus to design workable assessment plans. The press for assessment certainly suggests it as an area in which scholars interested in faculty development can specialize.

Faculty Development Support for Assessment of Teaching and Learning

Faculty development has historically focused on meeting the needs of individual faculty members (Sorcinelli et al., 2006) as a primary goal and meeting institutional needs as a secondary goal. With many institutions seeking ways to enhance student learning and ensure that more students achieve academic success, teaching and learning centers are a natural source for providing expertise concerning assessment of student learning. As noted in Chapter 4, assessment of student learning outcomes is indeed a top issue that faculty developers address through programming (see Table 4.1). Furthermore, it is the top issue developers identified for the field to address in the next five years (see Table 6.1) and the most prevalent issue developers noted when discussing the future directions in which faculty development should and will move in the next decade (see Chapter 6). Respondents also indicated that fewer than 20% of the assessment offices at their institutions (if such an office exists) independently offer professional development programming to support faculty engagement in assessment (see Table 2.3); thus, the field appears to be open for faculty developers to take a leadership role. In fact, slightly more than half (54%) of centers collaborate with assessment offices on their campuses to offer that support.

Developers in this current study reported a variety of ways in which they are involved with assessment of student learning. The quantitative findings and open-ended comments indicate that developers are committed to and actively engaged in helping faculty learn how to assess their students' learning and how to use the results to improve their teaching. Typically, developers see themselves as coaches and resources to help instructors build their own skills as assessors, rather than putting themselves in the role of assessors of student learning. The following comment from a liberal arts assistant/associate director reflects developers' commitment to approaches that support instructors without directing them:

> Faculty development efforts can be uniquely poised to fold assessment best practices into teaching and learning support and resources—done in such a way that feels useful and collegial to faculty rather than top-down/heavy handed/pointless.

In the spirit of being mentors or coaches, developers see the need to help faculty integrate assessment into their overall teaching approaches and to help them understand and follow a full assessment cycle: integrating measurable/discernable outcomes into syllabi, planning meaningful and authentic assessments of those outcomes, and using the data from those assessments to improve their practice. A compelling vision for how that can be achieved was offered by a director at a comprehensive university whose comments show understanding of the challenges of helping others wrestle with the complex and nuanced issues that relate to good teaching as well as to assessment processes.

> In cross-disciplinary groups, [we can] help faculty learn more about the epistemology of their fields. What is difficult for students to learn (threshold concepts)? What do experts do so they do not get stuck (decoding the disciplines)? With their unconscious competence decoded, it is now possible to show faculty how to model, provide practice, and assess student mastery of the bottlenecks to learning. The landscape for each field can be laid out in this manner, making it easier to tie the curriculum together and then use evidence-based learning to measure teaching and learning outcomes.

Commitment to supporting faculty in the work of assessing student learning, however, was not without accompanying concerns. Despite, or perhaps because of, this commitment to supporting faculty as they become adept at student assessment, developers expressed concern that the role of faculty as student learning assessors could ultimately diminish faculty commitment to professional growth, as some believe has happened in the K–12 arena. One developer expressed well what many noted:

> It is important for the overall health of higher education that faculty development programs avoid the trap into which secondary education fell, that is, becoming so focused on student assessment and student as client that the professors lack the time and opportunity to invest in their areas of expertise. It's a balancing act, to be sure, because no one wants a return to the sage on the stage. (Research/doctoral, instructional consultant/designer/coordinator)

Another concern identified by some developers pertained to potential implications of the assessment movement. Specifically, they were concerned with the tension between meaningful versus mechanical assessment: what truly captures the most important outcomes we wish our students to achieve rather than what is easy to measure. Similarly, some recognized the differences between creative approaches (involving authentic, triangulated assessment using multiple measures) versus prescriptive approaches to assessing student learning (involving standardized or single-outcome measures). As mentioned in Chapter 6, developers fear that prescriptive approaches to assessment will "suck the joy out of this work" for faculty and for themselves if they are, as one respondent noted, "forced to report what is easy to count instead of what is important to value."

Developers are in a strong position, because of their knowledge base and their increasingly central role in institutions, to influence the conversation about how assessment can and should be framed on campuses and how faculty fit into the larger picture. Some perceive that if assessment of student learning is the domain of faculty development, and the data generated on it reside in centers, developers would have greater influence on how such data are used. Even if centers do not take a leading role in assessing student learning, they can support faculty members as they individually engage in this work. The words of a respondent serving as an instructional consultant/designer/coordinator in a research and doctoral institution capture the important role for developers as expectations expand for faculty responsibility and accountability in assessing student learning outcomes:

> Universities will be forced to be accountable for student learning outcomes, in addition to research and engagement. Faculty development will need to respond by helping faculty.

The Role of Faculty Development in the Assessment of Faculty Work

Faculty developers are deeply committed to their roles in helping faculty assess student learning. They are less enthusiastic about taking on roles as evaluators of faculty worth or impact. Historically, the domains of responsibility in faculty development have not included evaluation of faculty work. That is, while they have supported faculty members in becoming more effective at their teaching, developers have tended to be firm about the separation of support for faculty professional growth activities from efforts to assess faculty work. Center leaders have often been willing to provide letters at the request of faculty members to confirm their involvement in center activities and programs but have eschewed any role as evaluators of quality teaching. The rationale has been that centers need to be safe spaces for faculty members to seek support and to experiment with new teaching approaches without concern about whether their efforts to improve could be used, through evaluation processes, in ways that could negatively affect their career, advancement, or remuneration opportunities.

In the current study, responses suggest that some developers are worried about threats to this long-recognized separation of growth from evaluation. Specifically, developers are concerned about being called on to assess faculty instructional quality. Some expressed concern about the implications for faculty members and for themselves as developers if the results of their efforts to support assessment of student learning outcomes should be tied to decisions about tenure and promotion. One faculty member at a research institution saw worrisome implications for faculty development because of "the managerial push for assessment of learning outcomes, along with the demands from society for efficacy in higher education." Another developer noted that assessment and student degree completion mandates may dictate the directions faculty development takes.

Although they are not interested in assuming roles as evaluators of faculty performance, developers would support new criteria that emphasize evidence of assessment of student learning as part of a well-developed reflective teaching portfolio. As discussed, some developers indicated that they could help faculty members build skills and processes to integrate self-assessment into their work and that evidence from such assessment might be included in teaching portfolios. Others expressed a lack of confidence that the criteria institutions develop would reflect the depth and complexity involved in teaching. Further, the expectations of such criteria in the tenure and promotion process add a layer of responsibility on faculty members, many of whom might be unable to address this new complexity.

Although developers are not sanguine about direct involvement in evaluation of faculty work, they tend to see SoTL as a way to engage faculty meaningfully and creatively in the examination of their own teaching and their students' learning at the same time that they produce the kind of data being sought for program improvement and accreditation. Although SoTL was not a top service offered (see Table 5.1), nor a signature service for any institutional types except for Canadian institutions (see Table 5.2), it was the top service directors wished to expand overall. Furthermore, support for SoTL was mentioned often in the open-ended comments about future directions in which the field should move. Developers' ideas for SoTL are best represented in the following comment from a director in a liberal arts college:

> I wrote that I think the field should move toward a scholarship of teaching and learning but will likely move toward accreditation and assessment of student learning outcomes. In a way, these two areas are similar. The difference for me is internal [versus] external motivation. I would love to see faculty developers actually leading a movement that helps more faculty study their own teaching and their students' learning because they want to, rather

than trying to get them to comply with accrediting bodies' demands for assessment plans. It seems that faculty could collect the same data and put in the same amount of work, and satisfy both themselves and the accrediting bodies, if they did the first.

Several developers noted the differences between SoTL that is internally motivated and proactively pursued and an externally motivated or mandated assessment of individuals and programs for accreditation. They hoped the field of faculty development could encourage internally motivated SoTL efforts and could avoid the latter. However, they were not confident about the ability of institutions to do so. One instructional consultant in a research university expressed concern that demands from accreditation bodies and other pressures for assessment would lead to "shallow approaches to assessment rather than the deep investigation offered by SoTL and other more scholarly approaches to teaching."

Overall, developers strongly support opportunities for faculty members to reflect on their teaching and their students' learning but do not want their work reduced to evaluating instructors' teaching for institutional action. They also do not want their support of faculty assessment of their own teaching and their students' learning narrowed to institutionally mandated measures. Although they do not see themselves involved in direct ways in evaluating faculty work, developers can see roles for themselves in supporting faculty members as they self-evaluate, prepare portfolios for evaluative purposes, or engage in the SoTL that produces findings useful to ongoing improvement or as evidence for evaluation purposes.

Faculty Development to Support Institutional Assessment and Accreditation

As noted earlier in this chapter, the traditional approach to faculty development has been formative, voluntary, faculty driven, and based on faculty needs (Austin, 2010; Sorcinelli et al., 2006). The accreditation agenda that is increasingly propelling institutional decision-making is summative, nonvoluntary, externally driven, and based on the need for evidence of educational outcomes and institutional improvement. Further, the field of faculty development has been committed to the values of confidentiality and privacy in its work with faculty and in keeping a firewall between the work conducted with faculty for their own improvement (whether individual consultation or group initiatives such as FLCs or SGIDs) and work for institutional decision-making. We are beginning to see more explicit linkages between the improvement of student learning and the development of instructors who facilitate such learning in at least one accreditation body (i.e., Quality Enhancement Plan [QEP], which is discussed later). For many developers, however, an inherent tension remains between assisting with assessment in service of the faculty and supporting accountability in service of the institution. This tension is evident in developers' open-ended comments about institutional learning outcomes assessment and involvement with institutional accrediting agencies.

Developers understand the need for course and program-level assessment for institutional improvement and for accreditation. Still, the quantitative survey data are not sufficient to make claims that this agenda is of growing importance in the field. Most of the questions pertaining to program-level assessment or support for accreditation are new in the current survey, and so there are no comparative data from the 2006 study. In the current study, however, it is clear that helping the institution respond to accreditation and supporting QEP are not among the goals most salient to directors (see Table 2.1), and program assessment is not among the top issues developers report addressing (see Table 4.1), nor among the issues they identify for expansion (see Table 4.3) and attention in the next five years (see Table 6.1). Developers' qualitative reflections on institutional assessment and accreditation, however, offer a nuanced and complex understanding of the potentials and pitfalls of greater engagement with assessment needs beyond services that focus on assisting faculty in diagnosing and improving their own teaching practices and their students' learning.

One future direction faculty developers suggested for the field is an acknowledgment of the potential synergy achievable when responding to department-level needs in conjunction with individual faculty needs. Some developers advocated for a more explicit linkage among individual course-based assessment and program-level curriculum revision and review. A program coordinator at a comprehensive university noted the potential of "teaching the processes of course and curriculum design as a method for improving interest and compliance in/with assessment (for accreditation)." A director at a community college echoed this idea:

> [We should] increasingly move toward program-level curriculum development support (including the assessment of program learning outcomes)—which also leads to just-in-time faculty development with all members of academic units (not just those who would otherwise come to the center). Due to resource constraints, faculty development needs to become more strategic in aligning its work with the needs of faculty and academic units.

Other developers envisioned a future for the field in which there will be greater collaboration among units working on assessment or accreditation with the addition of assessment responsibilities and projects in centers. A senior-level administrator at a research and doctoral university stated in a comment regarding where the field should go, "I think there has to be even more collaboration and combination of faculty development, assessment, and accreditation. All of these issues need to be working together and not in separate spheres. I am excited about that." This administrator followed up with where the field will likely go by suggesting that such collaboration could also bring more resources to teaching centers: "I think adding assessment and accreditation to faculty development is pedagogically sound and I think it will help centers and funding for development survive." Finally, a respondent pointed out that developers have additional opportunities to shape approaches to assessment:

> Accreditation . . . is an essential function on all campuses and we bring relevant expertise (but working the developmental aspects of accreditation—the data collection aspect for the purpose of grounding decisions in order to keep improving—don't want to fall into summative processes altogether). (Research/doctoral, associate/assistant director)

Perhaps the best example of the sentiments expressed by the several developers who believe that faculty development will move in the direction of greater assistance with assessment, institutional research, and accreditation initiatives is offered in the advice of a senior-level administrator at a research/doctoral institution:

> Faculty development would be well served by keeping knowledgeable and connected with these agendas for change—understanding how institutions work (OD) [organizational development], multiple ways to assess faculty needs, departmental needs—and figure out the required balance between them—understanding the central administration/institutional needs and responding (with caution as well as enthusiasm, depending on the need).

We want to note that although the comments about faculty developers' involvement in supporting institutional assessment needs were generally positive or neutral, reflecting what they see as a "new reality," some developers expressed concern about the larger context in which that involvement takes place. As a director at a research/doctoral institution said, "I think without strong leadership that provides a compelling vision of higher education as something more than a means to economic success, faculty development will be drawn further toward supporting the assessment and commodification of knowledge and learners."

Developers' key concerns regarding institution-level assessment and accreditation revolve around their role in maintaining the field's commitment to voluntary, confidential engagement with faculty. They see the need to balance those principles with press to make public data that provides evidence of teaching, learning and program outcomes. Developers see the opportunity for external forces to catalyze institutional change approaches that meaningfully engage faculty; one of the strongest concerns expressed was that institutional responses would miss this opportunity.

As the Age of Evidence emerges, there may be positive news on the institutional assessment and accreditation front. We are beginning to see the possibility for accreditation to include enhancement of educational quality and improvement of the effectiveness of institutions. As of this writing, the Southern Association of Colleges and Schools (SACS) is unique among U.S. accreditation bodies in its requirement for colleges and universities to develop QEPs. Guidelines for the QEP state that it should include "a process identifying key issues emerging from institutional assessment" and should focus "on learning outcomes and/or the environment supporting student learning and accomplishing the mission of the institution" (SACS, 2015). The QEP thus focuses the use of evaluation data on improving student learning outcomes (Sorcinelli & Garner, 2013). Practical responses to the QEP requirement have been as varied as the institutions that developed them, but many have been developed with substantial input and, in some cases, coleadership from teaching and learning centers (Sorcinelli & Garner, 2013). While approaches to the QEP obviously differ depending on institutional type, they are all bound by a focus on student learning rather than on institutional goals and resources.

Conclusion

Faculty development on assessment of student learning outcomes is robust and diverse and is a top priority in current programming and in future directions for the field. Faculty development on assessment of teaching and academic programs for accreditation is less prevalent and not reported as a priority. Developers see it on the horizon and include it in their discussion of future directions. The challenge for developers in their institutions and in the larger field will be to shape the assessment frameworks so they reflect the complexity and diversity of teaching and learning, academic programs, and institutional missions.

It is clear from the current study that those in the field of faculty development need and want to prioritize discussions about assessment and its use in evidence-based practice in the near term and in the long term. The tensions identified by developers in addressing the potentially incompatible needs of individual faculty and of institutions, as well as in deciding the frameworks of assessment, call for wide-ranging discussion and research. Likewise, developers need to discuss the scope of possibilities for assessing the impact of their own work. Faculty developers, no longer at the margins but in the thick of institutional planning, have an opportunity to use their expertise to shape how assessment is implemented throughout their institutions and how they themselves model best practices. In this hopeful future, we envision that faculty developers increasingly will be called on to broaden the scope of their engagement in meaningful assessment and to create networks with faculty and institutional leaders to respond to institutional problems with constructive solutions. We see faculty developers becoming associated even more clearly than at present with an institutional commitment to excellence and an environment that supports student learning and the instructors who facilitate such learning. This, for us, is the essence of the Age of Evidence.

Chapter Highlights

- In the emerging Age of Evidence, assessment will play an increasingly prominent role in the practice and priorities for faculty developers.
- The scope of work that faculty developers report regarding assessment of student learning is broad, and the topic is a top current service and future priority for the field. Developers see SoTL as a key approach to helping faculty learn to integrate assessment into their teaching practices in meaningful ways.
- Academic program assessment and support for accreditation is not among the current services faculty developers generally offer, would expand if given the opportunity, or see as a priority for the field to address in the next five years. Developers' perspectives on the need to support assessment for institutional goals emerge in the open-ended comments about longer-term directions of the field.
- Faculty developers understand the need to support course and program-level assessment for institutional improvement and for accreditation. They are generally matter-of-fact or positive about the field moving in that direction. Their caveats are a concern that doing so does not compromise the field's long-standing commitments to voluntary and

confidential work with faculty, and that the frameworks adopted for such assessment meaningfully engage faculty for their own benefit as much as for the institution's benefit.

- Faculty developers are acutely aware of the need to assess the quality and impact of their own programs. They are actively engaged in tracking participation in and satisfaction with their programs but are challenged in assessing their impact on instructional practice or on student learning.

8

WHAT HAVE WE LEARNED?

As we discussed in detail in Chapter 1, the national landscape of higher education has changed in the past decade. Pressures for cost-effectiveness, federal interest in competitiveness of U.S. graduates on a global stage, and national interest by multiple stakeholders in student success have led to increased interest in teaching and learning outcomes, effective teaching practices, and the assessment of both. A sharp rise in technologies that support blended, hybrid, and online courses offers higher education institutions new opportunities to expand their reach beyond their campus walls, from undergraduate courses that serve students with hectic schedules to hybrid international graduate programs and massive open online courses (MOOCs). The tenure-line faculty role is increasingly fragmented, and many courses are now taught by temporary or part-time instructors. All these forces, and others, have implications for faculty development in the Age of Evidence.

In this chapter we reexamine the concluding chapter of Sorcinelli, Austin, Eddy, and Beach (2006), which proposed that we were on the cusp of a new age—the Age of the Network. The chapter offered a working agenda that we believed could build on the Ages of the Scholar, Teacher, Developer, and Learner, and could provide useful guidance to faculty developers in planning for the future. We outlined seven interrelated priority areas for the field to consider moving forward:

1. Promoting the professional preparation of developers
2. Informing faculty development practice with scholarship
3. Broadening the scope of faculty development
4. Linking individual and institutional needs
5. Acknowledging the importance of context
6. Redefining *faculty diversity*
7. Recognizing faculty development as a shared responsibility

In the ensuing decade, faculty developers have made significant progress on many of those key priorities, but more remains to be done. In this concluding chapter we use the new data from this book to outline our perspectives on major imperatives that faculty developers will likely need to address in the coming decade and pose questions that we believe need to be addressed to meet those imperatives. As with our prior book, we envision that faculty development professionals can use this agenda to guide periodic reviews of their work and planning for the future, whereas senior institutional leaders will find it useful as a springboard for thoughtful analysis and discussion of faculty development as a strategic lever for enhancing institutional excellence. In the following sections, we revisit the recommendations we made, discuss the new findings in relation to those prior recommendations, and offer our perspectives on priorities moving forward.

Develop a Range of Paths Into the Profession

As a result of the 2006 study, we recommended that the field devote additional attention to and consideration of the role of faculty development professionals, including their preparation and career paths. We noted that a significant percentage of the field, particularly center directors, appeared to be quite new in their roles. We asked whether there was value in defining a set of core competencies or professional preparation for faculty development work. For that reason, in our current study we probed more deeply into the backgrounds and career pathways of developers to better understand the range and scope of disciplines and prior experiences developers bring to this work.

We found several themes in our study data as well as in the larger higher education landscape related to the route into (and out of) the profession that raise noteworthy questions. These themes include the imbalanced demographic profile of faculty developers compared to higher education faculty, the changing pathways into the profession, career choices that might unintentionally create roadblocks to future advancement in the field, and the influence of national associations in shaping the next generation of faculty developers.

As the faculty and the student bodies in most higher education institutions become more diverse on multiple dimensions, we might expect those working in the field of faculty development to match that diversity. Faculty developers, however, are predominantly aging, White, and female, a profile that does not align with the demographics of the overall faculty (Trower, 2012). Over many years, the POD Network has maintained a commitment to attract a diverse group of developers into the field, as evidenced by an active standing diversity committee, travel grants, and conference internships. These efforts have produced only modest results. But the future demographics of the field have the potential to be different. With 48% of the directors represented in this study at age 55 or older, the next decade presents an opportunity to actively and intentionally recruit, prepare, and support a diverse group of new developers and directors.

We suspect there are multiple reasons why women are overrepresented in the field and people of color are underrepresented. For example, in the past, faculty development positions may have offered an alternative career for women who, for lack of opportunity or by choice, did not pursue a traditional academic career involving advancement through the tenure track. Regarding the low representation of people of color, one might speculate that individuals from a range of different racial and ethnic groups may not have considered a career path in faculty development as sufficiently welcoming and receptive, particularly at predominantly White institutions. In fact, 75% of the small number of African American developers who responded to the survey are at an HBCU. This observation suggests that institutional culture and climate, more than the specific activities of the profession, may be a deterrent to faculty of color. The small number of non-White respondents in our current study does not allow us to make any conclusions. We can only identify a significant concern for the field going forward and call for serious attention to diversifying the profession. More research is needed to fully understand the reasons for the inequities in representation. However, evidence throughout this book supports developers' awareness of the need for the profession to parallel the diversity that is increasingly seen among the student bodies and faculties of higher education institutions.

A more pointed focus on the pathways individuals take to enter the field may be one way to diversify the profession (as well as to pave the way for replacing those who will be retiring in the next decade). It will be important to extend the preliminary scholarship on pathways to the profession (McDonald, 2010) to better identify the fields new developers might come from, highlight their career options and opportunities, clarify the professional competencies they need, and develop on-ramps and appropriate socialization and support. Our current study indicates that faculty developers predominantly emerge from the ranks of the faculty. Specifically, 35% of directors indicated that they held a faculty position immediately prior to their current one. Similar percentages of respondents in other positions, such as senior-level administrators, program coordinators, assistant or associate directors, and instructional consultants, also indicated that they had come directly from the faculty (Table 1.6). If one critical path to faculty development originates in the faculty ranks, institutional leaders as well as those in the field might consider explicit ways to target faculty members, especially from diverse groups, and provide them with opportunities for taking on formal faculty development roles. Some institutions already provide opportunities for faculty to serve as fellows or senior advisers in centers or to take on leadership roles for learning communities and other programs. More explicit institutional attention to identifying and attracting faculty members for these roles might be a strategy for preparing and diversifying the ranks of those who enter the field.

There is increasing interest among funding agencies (for example the National Science Foundation, and private foundations such as Andrew W. Mellon, Alfred P. Sloan, and Teagle) in course and curricular reform, teaching improvement, faculty development, and organizational change in support of undergraduate education. As a result, grant support from these agencies and faculty members in various disciplines (often in the STEM fields, especially at research universities) are becoming involved in faculty development projects and activities. Although historically faculty developers often came from the humanities, social sciences, and education, the representation from the STEM fields in faculty development has increased in recent years. At some universities, STEM scholars are taking on senior leadership roles in faculty development centers as well as leading grassroots faculty development initiatives. We project that with the growing interest in STEM education, more scientists, engineers, technology-focused scholars, and mathematicians may move into the profession. Because men currently dominate those fields, there may be a rebalancing of the predominance of women as well as shifts in the disciplinary areas most represented in the field.

With the growing importance of technology, assessment, brain science, and organizational development and change, new developers in the field will probably need a wide range of knowledge and skills. Another source of new developers might be from doctoral programs that are preparing professionals and scholars in fields such as higher education, disciplinary science education, instructional design and development, sociology, organizational development, and communications. Informal observation leads us to believe that a growing number of doctoral students in these programs are setting their sights on entering careers in faculty development directly from their graduate work. To prepare and encourage these early career professionals, faculty development leaders could explore ways to form partnerships with doctoral programs to offer internships and other opportunities for students to learn about the profession.

There is an important caveat to the suggestion of building a fast-track or at least a guided path from graduate school into faculty development. Only a small percentage (too small to report in Chapter 1) of developers in any current position indicate that their immediate prior position was graduate student. This finding suggests the possible risk of creating a bifurcated field in which instructional consultants and even assistant or associate directors are professionals who have joined centers directly from graduate work or other professional roles but who have limited upward mobility because they have not been faculty. They might have extensive experience consulting with faculty, creating programs, facilitating learning communities, and assessing the impact of their programs but can be ineligible or less attractive for assuming a director's role (or the role of associate provost). This situation could create stress in the field and diminish the attractiveness of the professional career path.

Emeritus faculty developers are another group to consider in regard to pathways into and out of the profession. Historically, most directors quietly retire from their centers and the POD Network. With a significant proportion of developers (particularly directors and senior leaders) nearing points of transition to retirement or a return to the faculty, those currently in the field need to consider how to retain access to the knowledge, experience, and wisdom emeritus developers can offer. At the same time, some former center directors and developers may not be ready to retire but rather may be midcareer professionals interested in moving on to other research, teaching, or leadership responsibilities. Keeping such professionals committed to and involved in the field, even if they are not in active faculty development work, should be of strategic importance to institutional leaders. These midcareer professionals can be champions and translators for those unfamiliar with faculty development and may be in key positions to advocate for and support its continued growth. Emeriti faculty developers, retiring and nonretiring, might be tapped as mentors for new developers and as ambassadors among their faculty colleagues to explain the value of the work.

As previously noted, the POD Network as an organization has worked for many years to identify ways to attract a diverse group of developers into the field. Yet, this study suggests that continued commitment and effort are needed to create a more diverse, inclusive, and professionally prepared field, ready to work with an increasingly diverse faculty. In 2006 we saw a strong concern over the *professionalization of the field*, defined as the creation of graduate programs to prepare faculty developers and the identification of a set of competencies expected of entry-, mid-, and senior-level professionals. Those concerned did not want to lose the sense of calling that faculty often express when moving into faculty development work. Comments gathered in the current study did not highlight concern about professionalization (perhaps because a graduate pathway does not appear to have developed in the past decade to any appreciable extent). However, given the increasingly complex set of skills needed to lead networked and evidence-based faculty development centers (discussed in later sections), the field would benefit from intentional engagement regarding the optimal skill sets needed in early career developers, in directors, and in the senior leaders who are emerging as a new group leading faculty development efforts on campuses. The field needs more detailed research on pathways into and out of faculty development. The POD Network could take a leadership role in such research. The Network can also undertake active outreach to disciplinary associations and promote faculty development as a career option. The recent interest in the disciplines on teaching and learning would make this outreach timely.

There is a compelling need for more detailed research about career pathways and ways to attract diverse professionals to those pathways. Key questions include the following:

- What plans and strategies might be developed in centers, institutions, and nationally to attract and retain a more diverse group of professionals in the field?
- What competencies and skills will professionals in the field need in the coming decade to work and lead evidence-based and networked faculty development centers?
- What alliances with graduate programs might be fostered to deepen the skill sets of current developers or to prepare the next generation of faculty developers?
- What research would be most important to support efforts to diversify the field and provide innovative and fruitful career progressions for faculty developers?
- Building on efforts already under way, what further roles might the POD Network play in helping to diversify the profession? How might the POD Network collaborate with colleagues in disciplinary associations and with leaders in the emerging STEM center movement to interest a range of colleagues in the opportunities for leadership in faculty development?

Inform Practice With Scholarship and Assessment

A decade ago, we urged the field to draw on scholarship in thoughtful, systematic, and meaningful ways to inform practice. We noted that historically faculty developers have used and contributed to the literature describing theory and scholarship on faculty careers and faculty work. Our recommendations at that time called for advances in building a body of scholarly work and expertise pertaining not only to teaching and learning and approaches to faculty development but also to organizational change and transformation. We also called on those in the field to consider how developers could most effectively disseminate their research to faculty members and institutional leaders as well as more broadly to the larger field of faculty development.

The data from the current study indicate significant advances and ongoing interest in the role of scholarship in informing practice. Assessment of student learning outcomes was among the top issues that developers indicated the field should address in the next five years (Table 6.1) and was among the top directions in which developers thought faculty development should and will move in the next decade. The comments presented in Chapters 6 and 7 illustrate developers' awareness that their historical role helping faculty assess student learning will be expanding in the future. They indicate the need to support institutional efforts to assess student learning, courses, and academic programs. The need to be systematic in assessing the impact of their own programs.

Faculty developers are certainly not alone in their awareness of the importance of informing practice with evidence. There is considerable interest across the higher education community in scholarship related to teaching and learning, faculty development, and organizational change in higher education. The emergence of discipline-based education research (DBER) scholars—those who identify with their disciplines while focusing specifically on issues of learning and pedagogy—has brought new perspectives and expertise into the field. In particular, DBER scholars often bring advanced research methods to (often funded) studies that deepen the nature of the evidence on important teaching and learning issues.

At the same time, nationally prominent leaders and organizations are calling for greater use of evidence to inform practice. One example is the National Science Foundation's Division of Undergraduate Education (DUE), which is providing extensive funding for projects to advance institutional change in support of undergraduate student learning, especially in STEM fields. DUE officials expect substantive research and evaluation designs in projects that are funded and provide resources and models to prospective grantees to guide those designs. Another example is the Teagle Foundation, which has sponsored outcomes and assessment grants to help liberal arts colleges create more coherent and intentional curricula with goals, pathways, and outcomes that are clear to students and other constituencies.

Various recent publications have highlighted the ways research can and should inform practice pertaining to teaching and learning, faculty development, and organizational change. Examples include the widely disseminated *Discipline-Based Education Research: Understanding and Improving Learning in Undergraduate Science and Engineering* (Singer, Nielsen, & Schweingruber, 2012) and *Reaching Students: What Research Says About Effective Instruction in Undergraduate Science and Engineering* (Kober, 2015), which provide specific and practical guidance to faculty about strategies to support deeper student learning. The work on the science of learning is also moving forward in great leaps, producing findings that shed new light on how students learn; the barriers that can thwart learning; and the instructional approaches most likely to be effective, and for whom. Just one example of such emerging work that draws from several disciplinary knowledge bases is Ludvik's (2016) *The Neuroscience of Learning and Development: Enhancing Creativity, Compassion, Critical Thinking, and Peace in Higher Education.*

Faculty developers themselves are contributing to, as well as benefitting from, this rapid stream of work influencing the field. Examples of this work include *Advancing the Culture of Teaching on Campuses: How a Teaching Center Can Make a Difference* (Cook & Kaplan, 2011); *Coming in from the Margins: Faculty Development's Emerging Organizational Development Role in Institutional Change* (Schroeder, 2010); *A Discipline-Based Teaching and Learning Center: A Model for Professional Development* (Marbach-Ad, Egan, & Thompson, 2015); *Faculty Development and Student Learning: Assessing the Connections* (Condon, Iverson, Manduca, Rutz, & Willett, 2016); *A Guide to Faculty Development* (Gillespie & Robertson, 2010); *Inside the Undergraduate Teaching Experience: The University of Washington's Growth in Faculty Teaching Study* (Beyer, Taylor, & Gillmore, 2013); and *Taking College Teaching Seriously: Pedagogy Matters!: Fostering Student Success Through Faculty-Centered Practice Improvement* (Mellow, Woolis, Kalges-Bombich, & Restler, 2015).

As noted in Chapter 7, we've characterized this emerging era as the Age of Evidence because of the press for evidence about the impact of faculty development efforts, coupled with the significant body of research providing new and useful findings about learning, teaching, and institutional environments that shape the student experience. This age brings exciting opportunities as well as challenges and questions about the role of assessment in faculty development practice. Although faculty developers usually track participation numbers and gather self-report data from their participants, they typically have not employed extensive assessment practices. Comments in the survey and the interviews indicate that directors are quite aware of the pressures on them to provide evidence of their impact. They are also aware of the challenges in conducting the thorough assessments they know would represent best practice. Research into assessment strategies could focus on those that are feasible within the time and resource constraints that are common for faculty development centers. Engaging faculty members in SoTL is one approach with strong support from developers who have significant knowledge of it. Developers also can encourage institutional commitment to regular, faculty-vetted, meaningful benchmarking and data collection regarding teaching practices and student learning. Because the research on the impact of effective teaching practices on student motivation and achievement is strong and consistent, faculty developers know which teaching methods are most effective and, therefore, can focus on how their centers' work affects the use of such evidence-based methods in their institutions.

Although these suggestions emphasize approaches that developers at a variety of institutional types with a range of resources might implement, some approaches to assessment of teaching and learning can require more sophisticated and advanced methodological expertise in evaluation and research design. When such specialized or additional expertise is needed, faculty developers might consider exploring resources available in their institution or in the surrounding region. As noted in Chapter 7, graduate students from a variety of disciplines may welcome the opportunity to practice their research skills and garner authorship on presentations and publications. Developers also can seek out other units on campus or consult with them to design workable assessment plans. Some institutions identify faculty or professional staff with relevant expertise who are interested in taking on special roles as assessment fellows.

In the Age of Evidence, assessment, evaluation, research findings, and student, instructor, and institutional data will play a critical role in the practice and advancement of faculty development. The following key questions deserve the attention of the field:

- How can developers play a central role in helping their institutions support evidence-based practice in teaching and learning?
- In what ways can developers efficiently and effectively assess the impact of the programs they offer? What methods and strategies are most promising and useful to the profession and to university and college leaders who need to make strategic decisions on the part of their institutions and faculty?
- How can faculty developers, those entering the field and those with much experience, ensure they have the skills and expertise in assessment and evaluation called for in the Age of Evidence?
- What might be the role of the POD Network in supporting the improvement of its members' practice with scholarship and assessment?

Broaden the Scope of Faculty Development

In 2006 we found that faculty developers focused primarily on issues of teaching and learning in regard to the goals driving their work and the services they offered. We recommended developers broaden the scope of their practice to address issues of organizational and institutional development, particularly in areas that have an impact on the teaching and learning enterprise, and of faculty roles across the career span. We connected this broader vision of faculty development to the changing roles of faculty and the need to support them as they integrate new responsibilities into their already challenging set of professional duties. In the Age of the Network, we argued, faculty developers should consider how they could collaborate with other units to identify gaps in support for faculty work and address them through shared efforts. Likewise, faculty developers could examine the extent to which their programs align with and support the mission of their institutions.

Since 2006 the landscape of faculty roles and institutional imperatives has broadened considerably. We have seen the array of technologies that have an impact on faculty work expand at astonishing rates (e.g., technologies to facilitate teaching and learning, platforms for virtual scholarly collaboration, and avenues for general communication). Online degrees have increased in number at traditional brick-and-mortar institutions, often challenging and shifting the teaching practices of faculty not previously trained or interested in teaching online. The literature is replete with studies on faculty perceptions about their experiences in this new educational arena. Further, producing peer-reviewed publications and obtaining grants has become far more competitive and more central to tenure and promotion at research and doctoral institutions and is seeping into the expectations at some master's-granting and liberal arts colleges. Institutions also face accreditation requirements to engage in thoughtful assessment of student learning outcomes, creating higher expectations on faculty and their departments for assessment at the course and program levels.

Our current findings support the fact that teaching and learning are still the core foci for faculty developers but that other issues have increased in importance. In Table 4.1, the top 10 services currently offered include a mix of teaching and learning (five issues), faculty work and development (three issues), and educational and institutional improvement (two issues). This is in contrast to our prior study, when new faculty development and institutional assessment of student learning outcomes were the only two services among the top 10 that addressed broader faculty and institutional issues. In addition, the services that directors are most interested in expanding are predominantly centered on elements of the faculty role beyond teaching and learning. These services include attending to the needs of different types of faculty (part-time, nontenure line) and at different career stages (mid-career and senior). Directors also see the need to expand educational and institutional development (including departmental leadership and management, assessment of student learning outcomes, course and curriculum reform, and general education reform; Table 5.3). Developers are noticeably thinking more broadly about who needs their support and what priorities they should address.

There is also evidence in our current study that faculty developers are not working in isolation in their centers but rather are networking with other units in their institutions, which we discuss more fully in a later section. They report fairly extensive collaboration with technology offices, college deans and associate deans, and libraries (Table 2.3), and lesser but still notable collaborations with assessment offices, graduate schools, and a variety of other units. This networking and collaboration crosses institutional types and center structures. We have no comparative data from 2006 to substantiate an increase in such collaborations, but we note that the scope of services in which directors reported being involved has increased over the decade.

Despite evidence that developers are broadening the scope of their services, they still strongly aspire to continue services and approaches that connect them to faculty and address issues of teaching and learning. The areas that developers identified as most urgent for the field to address in the near term are strongly related to teaching and learning, and the approaches they wish to expand involve extended work with faculty (e.g., FLCs, multiday institutes, and peer observation and feedback). Open-ended comments further corroborate developers' embrace of new expanded priorities as well as their wish to retain the core values and relationships that have been central to faculty development. The most eloquent of these comments speaks for many developers:

> I do see a continued need for one-on-one and small-group connections— consultation and learning communities. But faculty are so busy and the pace of life has changed so much from the early days of faculty development that I worry that the interpersonal connections and conversations about learning, teaching, and faculty life will be a challenge to sustain and centers will have to be more creative in figuring out how to do so.

The following important questions invite consideration as expectations for a broadened, networked, and evidence-based faculty development enterprise grow:

- How can developers balance traditional responsibilities and missions with new demands on their time and expertise?
- What planning strategies are fruitful for assisting center directors to establish priorities for their time and expertise?

- With whom, how, and to what extent are developers collaborating across their institutions to provide services, and how could such collaborations be enhanced?
- How can decisions about faculty development priorities and the use of resources be best connected with an analysis of institutional needs and the array of institutional resources?

Link Faculty and Institutional Needs

A decade ago, we discussed the need for faculty development efforts to link individual and institutional needs. We acknowledged that there was an expressed tension in our findings between focusing on the needs of individual faculty, including providing a safe haven as they strive to enhance their expertise as instructors, and addressing the specific priorities identified by institutional leaders. We argued that faculty developers who could be cognizant of both sets of needs and hold that tension in balance in their work would be well placed to positively influence institutional quality, responsiveness, creativity, and excellence.

In the 10 years since the first study, the press of outside forces (from legislatures, accreditors, and interest groups) has challenged the capacity of developers to address these multiple priorities. In 2006 the top goals guiding faculty developers' work aligned with their focus on teaching and learning and the interests of faculty: creating or sustaining a culture of teaching excellence, responding to individual faculty members' specific needs, and advancing new initiatives in teaching and learning. In our current survey, faculty developers reaffirmed their commitment to these goals but gave them different emphases: Creating and sustaining a culture of teaching excellence and advancing new initiatives in teaching and learning were still strongly identified, but responding to the needs of individual faculty members fell in importance. Developers also named being change agents in their institutions as a greater priority than fostering collegiality with and among faculty (see Table 2.1).

These shifting goals do not mean that developers are abandoning their commitment to individual faculty members. The services they report offering contain a balanced range of issues that are individually and institutionally focused. Developers' priorities for expansion include areas that arguably lie at the nexus of individual and institutional needs: support for part-time, non-tenure-track, and midcareer and late-career faculty. Responding to individual faculty needs for flexible, accessible resources and support for renewal and growth as instructors and scholars strengthens the institution and supports key institutional goals. At the same time, addressing course and curricular reform and departmental leadership strengthens the environment where individual faculty members work. Developers also expressed a commitment to continuing one-on-one consultations and individual relationships with instructors while simultaneously recognizing a need to find more creative ways to reach large numbers of faculty (especially part-time faculty) through online resources and Web-based programs. In assessing their own programs' impacts, they focused on feedback from individual participants, which is useful for needs assessment and program improvement, while also reporting such feedback as part of their communication with institutional stakeholders to demonstrate their impact.

We believe that these potentially competing commitments can and should be held in balance as the field moves ahead in the coming decade. Directors of centers with fewer resources may have to choose carefully the services they are best equipped to offer based on the expertise and background of the director and staff, while actively seeking collaborations with other units to ensure that the full spectrum of faculty and institutional priorities are met. Strategic decision-making about where to focus center resources and where to collaborate will be a feature of effective faculty development work. Directors will need to consider what organizational models are most useful to their unique situations. This imperative to prioritize and collaborate suggests the following questions for center leaders:

- What strategic planning approaches best help developers prioritize the needs of individual faculty members and the institution as a whole?
- What reflective planning approaches best help developers assess their own expertise and capacities, and how can developers incorporate those into the center's and institution's needs?
- In what ways can center leaders engage institutional leaders in setting priorities and goals that help balance multiple expectations and needs?
- How can center staff reach out to and involve leaders of other units in planning and collaboration in support of overall institutional goals relevant to faculty work?

Institutional Context Still Matters

Our original study determined that institutional type—research universities, comprehensive universities, liberal arts colleges, and community colleges—was central to understanding the variability of goals, structures, and issues that faculty developers addressed. What institution administrators valued, what constituted faculty work, and what developers focused on were mediated by institutional size, mission, resources, composition of the faculty, student body, and academic leadership. The study validated what developers already knew: Faculty development is not generic, nor is a single vision for the future of faculty development possible.

In 2006 the greatest commonality across institutional types could be found in the three primary goals for faculty development: to create a culture of teaching excellence, to respond to and support individual faculty members' goals for professional development, and to advance new initiatives in teaching and learning. In contrast, the organizational structures of faculty development, influences on practice, issues addressed through services, and future directions varied considerably by institutional type. We noted that the most widely recognized models, research, and practice tended to come from large research universities, and we encouraged more attention to the work of teaching centers at comprehensive universities, liberal arts colleges, and community colleges. Also, our familiarity with U.S. institutions was more robust than our knowledge of Canadian centers and the work of their faculty developers.

The current study documents a trend toward somewhat greater homogeneity than a decade ago. Respondents across institutional types all reported a substantial increase in more formalized structures for faculty development (centers and administrators rather than faculty committees and faculty with partial appointments), most markedly in liberal arts and community colleges (see Table 3.1). Also, developers across institutional types described similar foci in terms of the key issues addressed and approaches used to deliver services (see Tables 4.1 and 5.1). At the same time, nuances and distinctions among institutional types remain. The primary goals of centers appear more variable by institutional type than a decade ago, with developers in liberal arts and community colleges reporting a greater number of goals for their centers that support faculty interests and institutional needs, whereas research and comprehensive universities report fewer goals that are more focused on institutional change (see Table 2.2). The profiles of centers at different institutional types, in terms of staff levels and operating budgets, also vary in interesting ways. Centers across institution types face constrained resources (particularly comprehensive universities; see Table 3.5), but budgets and staff do vary, and patterns are discernable. Directors at different institutional types also report varied sources of supplemental program funds related to the missions of the institutions and their support of the pursuit of particular external funds (e.g., liberal arts college directors' access to private foundation funds and research directors' access to federal grants).

Looking beyond our own data to the larger higher education landscape, more attention has been given to faculty development in relation to institutional context over the past decade. Special interest groups in the POD Network, some organized by institutional type (e.g., POD Small College Committee), have flourished. Chapters in the most current guide to faculty development are organized by institutional type (Gillespie & Robertson, 2010), and recent publications on teaching centers in research universities and small colleges have added to the overall knowledge base (Cook & Kaplan 2011; Reder, 2014). Also, the international attention to SoTL (e.g., International Society for the Scholarship of Teaching and Learning Conference) and the availability of regional teaching conferences and consortia (e.g., Lilly Conferences on College Teaching) have given voice to and connected faculty from a wide variety of institutions. The potential synergies of these initiatives are formidable, and we believe the POD Network has the capacity to harness those synergies through its outreach efforts, joint conferences, and special issues of journals. We also welcome further analysis and interpretation of results from this current study, especially from faculty developers at community colleges and Canadian institutions.

Increasingly, administrators across institutional types recognize the need for more faculty professional development opportunities, and many of those administrators may have backgrounds that intersect with faculty development. As faculty development becomes formalized across institutional types through centers and designated individuals and is seen as a strategic lever for improving teaching and helping to raise student outcomes, developers may be tasked with additional work ("The center can take care of that"). Centers in every institutional type may end up with an unanticipated array of tasks and face the potential challenge of blurred missions and foci. Also, as faculty development becomes more centralized programs may lose some autonomy, which was a positive aspect of what scholars in the field referred to as being *on the margins* (Schroeder, 2010). Centers across institutional types are now far more in the spotlight or on the radar, and therefore will need to anticipate requests for institutionally driven initiatives and evidence of effectiveness. The trade-off for centrality and influence is reliance and accountability. In the coming decade directors at all institutional types plan on being closer to the center.

Budget constraints remain a significant issue across institutional types (see Table 3.6). Some centers are being asked to look for external funds or take on special projects or cost sharing with other units. Although funding is important at all institutions, directors from comprehensive universities and community colleges report the most constrained budgetary situations and often have limited resources to support grant-seeking or other entrepreneurial activities. In the past, center directors might not have been expected to have a savvy understanding of or considerable competency with money flow, budgets, how to negotiate for funds, and how to apply for external grants or internal special project funds. This may be a required skill set in the future.

Several important questions about institutional context invite further consideration:

- In what ways will faculty development priorities and strategies contract or diversify by institutional type? What will these movements mean for the skill set needed to successfully lead them?
- How can the POD Network prepare developers for issues and responsibilities that relate to all institutional contexts while also fostering ongoing research and recognition of the importance of particularity in institutional context in shaping faculty development?
- How might faculty developers acquire training in financial management, budget negotiation, and grant-seeking? What is the responsibility of the POD Network in supporting developers in this relatively new arena?

Promote an Expansive Definition of *Faculty Diversity*

In our 2006 study, we posed a series of questions to faculty developers regarding the extent to which they serve various types of faculty members (e.g., early career, midcareer, or senior faculty; tenure stream or tenured faculty; nontenure stream, contingent, part-time, and adjunct faculty; faculty of color; international faculty; department chairs). Our questions focused on the increasing diversity of faculty and students and its implications on the growth of faculty development associations as multicultural organizations. Many of those questions are still relevant and are addressed elsewhere in this chapter.

The findings of our current study indicate that over the past decade, academic career stage and faculty appointment type have garnered our attention. For example, the leading issue for which faculty development programs are providing services is new faculty development and orientation. New and early career faculty programs also garner the top position as a signature service of teaching centers (see Tables 4.1 and 4.2). In addition, at least to a *slight* to *moderate extent*, faculty developers are providing mentoring programs for underrepresented faculty; support and orientation for part-time, adjunct, and fixed-term faculty; and development opportunities for midcareer and senior faculty (see Table 4.1). The current findings reveal that directors strongly believe their centers should be offering more access and services to these constituencies, especially midcareer and senior faculty, underrepresented faculty, faculty preparing for departmental leadership, and part-time or adjunct faculty. Examples of such programs are presented in Chapter 4 and Chapter 5 among developers' signature services and approaches.

Developers' efforts to support faculty in a range of appointments are well reasoned; the reality is that almost three-quarters of faculty members today are not on a tenure track. Part-time instructors in particular face an array of teaching and faculty development challenges: limited or no experience in teaching at the particular type of institution; often no office hours for advising and mentoring students; and typically little input on institutional discussions about learning goals, course assignments, or textbook selection (Kezar, 2012). In recent studies, adjunct, part-time, and other contingent faculty also report limited access to faculty professional development (Eagan, Stolzenberg, Lozano, Aragon, Suchard, & Hurtado, 2014). Although these faculty members indicate a strong commitment to their teaching and a desire for professional development, they deem the professional development available to them as minimal. This may be why developers in the current study express an interest in adding just-in-time, widely available faculty development approaches such as high-quality asynchronous online programs, webinars, and Web-based resources to their center portfolios.

The past 10 years have also been marked by increased concerns about and responsiveness to the development of future faculty, not only at the institutional level also but at the national level. One example in the national landscape is the Center for the Integration of Research, Teaching, and Learning (CIRTL; www.cirtl.net) and its mission to prepare doctoral students in STEM fields to have the knowledge and skills to promote learning for a diverse range of students. CIRTL provides professional development, including a MOOC on teaching strategies and online workshops that is open to doctoral students studying in its 46-member universities and learning communities at each participating institution. Across the country, interest in preparing future faculty is sometimes situated in teaching centers; in other situations, faculty developers are working collaboratively with their graduate schools and academic colleges.

The end of the faculty career is also drawing attention. Many faculty members wish to remain connected with their institutions postretirement; the question is how to provide scaffolds to support continuity during the retirement transition, especially in regard to faculty engagement with the intellectual and social community (Baldwin & Zeig, 2012). In the same way that teaching centers are involved in first-year faculty mentoring and seminar programs, they may be asked to support or provide advice on retirement transition mentoring programs or emeritus FLCs. Administrators will have to find strategies to meet their own needs as well as the needs of an older faculty, especially with an aging academic workforce, no mandatory retirement age, and a growing reluctance of faculty to retire at the traditional age of 65 (Van Ummersen, McLaughlin, & Duranleau, 2014). Some institutions are already starting to take notice of this fifth generation of faculty, which is poised for retirement and a major shift in their identity.

In addition to responding to the range of faculty appointment types and career stages, developers continue to reflect on how they can strengthen diversity among the faculty. In a chapter on diversity, Bierwart (2012) outlines six significant ways that teaching centers can contribute most to diversity work. The chapter also includes a helpful template for analyzing the impact of multicultural faculty development work. Other publications, some by faculty developers themselves, have further highlighted the ways practices pertaining to diversity can be enhanced. Examples of scholarship on diversity in teaching, learning, and faculty development include *Black Faculty in the Academy: Narratives for Negotiating Identity and Achieving Career Success* (Bonner, Marbley, Tuitt, Robinson, Banda, & Hughes, 2014); *Cultural Diversity and Education: Foundations, Curriculum, and Teaching* (Banks, 2015); *Diversity and Motivation: Culturally Responsive Teaching in College* (Ginsberg & Wlodkowski, 2009); *Teaching for Diversity and Social Justice* (Adams & Bell, 2016); *Mentoring Faculty of Color: Essays on Professional Development and Advancement in Colleges and Universities* (Mack, Watson, & Camacho, 2012); and *Scholarship of Multicultural Teaching and Learning* (Kaplan & Miller, 2007).

Any expansion of center foci in these directions—appointment type, career stage, and diversity—will merit thoughtful exploration, development, and assessment of resources by center directors. Questions for faculty developers and teaching centers include the following:

- How can developers ascertain the needs of and respond to diverse constituencies in the institution?
- What new resources might centers need to support a particular group of faculty, or diverse groups across the range of domains (e.g., faculty of color; new, midcareer, and late career; different disciplines; part-time and fixed term)?
- What structures, services, and approaches to serving the full diversity of instructors will best suit the local institutional context? What collaborations with other units can centers create to achieve larger aims for supporting diverse faculty?
- In what ways can centers embody and reflect the knowledge, skills, and values that promote multicultural learning throughout the institution?
- What are the implications of an increasingly diverse faculty and student body for the growth of the POD Network as a multicultural organization?

Envision Faculty Development as Everyone's Work

A decade ago, in concluding our earlier book (Sorcinelli et al., 2006), we called for a wider perspective on who is responsible for faculty development, seeing it as work that is strategically important to the whole campus and requiring the talents of colleagues from across units. We suggested that the work of the faculty, and institutional support for that work, requires input from such entities as student affairs, the graduate school, the research office, and the assessment office. We mused that faculty developers might take on the roles of resource experts or coordinators who understand and can direct faculty to a range of resources. Recognizing that faculty development needs to be situated as a central institutional role in broader organizational activities, we asserted that the field was entering the Age of the Network. We also urged faculty developers to envision a role for themselves in facilitating collaborative, community work that is strategically important to the fulfillment of institutional goals.

In the subsequent years, our prediction about a shift toward shared ownership of faculty development has been borne out. More than half of the directors across institutional types reported collaborating with technology centers, academic deans, libraries, and assessment offices. More modest, but still noteworthy, collaborations have been occurring with community and service-learning centers, writing centers, offices for diversity and multiculturalism, and teaching assistant development programs. Directors also report that some of these units offer support and programs to faculty independently.

Networks are still important in the emerging Age of Evidence. In fact, networking, collaborating, and creating communities around shared goals may be more important than ever as universities and colleges are urged by multiple stakeholders to heighten their commitment to and success in supporting student learning and to provide evidence of the impact of their efforts. We have heard campus leaders call for new organizational mechanisms and cultural norms that diminish the strength of what some have seen as metaphorical silos on campuses, that is, offices and units that function with little cross-unit connection. Those who want to create new cultures call for bridges, pathways, neighborhoods, and communities that link offices and individuals with mutually supporting goals. Bryk, Gomez, Grunow, and LeMahieu (2015) studied the impact of networks and how to use such networks to improve education. Such research shows that real institutional transformation that leads to deeper learning and more successful students requires input, support, and collaborative effort from multiple sources across and beyond campus.

In this context, we call for renewed commitment to approaching faculty development as everyone's work. Universities and colleges will be best positioned to meet their goals of educational excellence if they draw on a full range of resources to support the growth, development, and success of the faculty. Thus, the expertise and knowledge from a range of offices are needed to meet the goals that developers in this study see as most urgent. Colleagues in writing centers, international offices, student health and counseling centers, libraries, educational technology, graduate schools, student affairs, and elsewhere are potential allies who can contribute to faculty development initiatives.

Decades ago, Gaff (1975) pointed out that in the final analysis, faculty development programs will be judged by their effect on student learning. Students should be more centrally involved in faculty development programs because they are the recipients of the changes stimulated by such efforts. They may not be experts in evaluating curriculum or pedagogy, but they are experts in their own experiences. Such partnerships could offer a fresh perspective on student success, bringing together units that serve students as well as faculty, and creating linkages among those diverse communities.

As they continue to address the tasks presented by the Age of the Network as well as the related tasks of the Age of Evidence, faculty developers face exciting and challenging questions. One of the most interesting concerns which models for collaboration and connectivity are the most promising. One approach would be to see teaching and learning centers as the hub of a wheel that includes a range of other offices as related spokes. In this approach, the faculty development center may take on the role of concierge, helping faculty members determine their needs and interests and then connecting them with the appropriate resources on campus. Another approach would be to see teaching and learning centers as equal partners in a loose network of related resources, sometimes under the purview of an associate provost for teaching and learning; this model is emerging with increasing frequency, especially at larger institutions.

The development of decentralized specialty centers that address specific needs and interests is another trend in an increasing number of large universities. Centers located in colleges of science or engineering, or even more specific to single disciplines, are the most prominent example of this trend. They may work separately or side by side with traditional centers for teaching and learning but with their own agendas, directors, and staff. This approach taps into the expertise of DBER scholars and the growing number of faculty in STEM fields taking on significant projects in educational innovation. Such STEM-related centers can find support through an organization called STEM Central, whose mission is to offer "a database of resources and network of communities working to improve and transform undergraduate STEM education in the United States" (STEM Central, n.d., para. 1). The

STEM Central website emphasizes its community-based approach, bringing together "educators, scientists, administrators, student support specialists, funders, and evaluators" (para. 1).

Each of these models offers possibilities for expanding institutional attention to teaching and learning, supporting faculty members as instructors, and encouraging faculty to be institutional change agents. The strengths and limitations of these models in different institutional contexts remain items worthy of research and evaluation in coming years. In addition to questions about structure, various related questions also deserve consideration.

- What kind of leadership issues need attention as faculty development becomes more connected, collaborative, and networked?
- How can the next generation of developers be best prepared for working in the Age of the Network and the Age of Evidence? What personal perspectives, disciplinary expertise, and experiential backgrounds would lend themselves to professional excellence among those entering a networked and connected world?
- How can the POD Network support faculty development collaboration with other units on campuses through national outreach to other associations and societies that represent them?

Concluding Thoughts

The findings of our 2006 study validated our belief that faculty development is a critically important lever for ensuring institutional excellence. We observed that as the context for higher education changed and faculty members assumed new roles and responsibilities, faculty development professionals and senior leaders were addressing the question of the place of faculty development in the institutional landscape. We questioned whether in the future faculty development would be a useful but marginal resource, or whether it would be conceptualized and organized in ways that made it central to individual faculty members' growth and institutional quality, health, and excellence. Based on the current study, we conclude that faculty development is now more central and widely recognized as an important support for teaching and learning and a key lever for change in higher education institutions. We draw this conclusion not only from our research, detailed in this book, but also from our practice in our institutions and our work with colleagues nationally. We see faculty developers engaged in and beyond their own campuses in myriad ways: as principal and coprincipal investigators on grant projects funded by the National Science Foundation, the U.S.

Department of Education, and private foundations; as consultants to other institutions whose administrators seek to build stronger supports for faculty; and in interdisciplinary teams of change agents focused on student success, campus classroom building projects, general education reform, tenure and promotion policy, and educational technology implementation.

As we were finishing this book, Austin and Sorcinelli attended the conference Defining the New Normal, sponsored by the Alfred P. Sloan Foundation and hosted by Harvard University. The goals of the conference were to create an emerging definition of a *new normal* in higher education—a future in which college and university teaching practices will align with what we know about how people learn—and identify possible road maps to change that move toward that new normal (Slakey & Gobstein, 2015).

What was significant about this event is that directors and staff from teaching and learning centers were not simply invited to the table; they were central to the conference agenda and dialogue. The conference brought together several different groups: the directors of the Ivy Plus centers for teaching and learning; representatives from multi-institutional, higher education reform-minded communities including the American Association of Universities, the Bay View Alliance, CIRTL, the Council of Graduate Schools; and representatives of the National Science Foundation, the Andrew W. Mellon Foundation, the Howard Hughes Medical Institute, and the Teagle Foundation. Also included were faculty with varying administrative roles who shared their perspectives on the challenges and opportunities for bringing about the new normal being conceptualized.

The discussion that ensued confirmed for us the salience of the trends, imperatives, and questions we have discussed throughout this chapter. The envisioned new normal focused on students, faculty, and faculty development. It sees students as more intentional, connected, and engaged through bridging cocurricular and curricular spaces and scaffolding learning across a lifetime, turning students into cocreators of knowledge and agents in their own learning. The new normal would fully embrace a diverse faculty engaged in teaching that is reflective and intentional, assessment for continuous improvement of their courses, and evaluation of teaching that is meaningful and counts in tenure and promotion. It would include shared discourse among faculty and administrators, partnerships with a range of stakeholders, a reward structure that measures and values teaching, and intergenerational mentoring throughout an institution.

Faculty development in the new normal would build networks, communities, coalitions, and hubs. Developers would be conveners, aggregators, and surveyors, knowing the landscape, bringing people together, and being visible. They would serve as translators of research and relevant scholarship into evidence-based practices, decoders of the interests of academic leaders and faculty, and finders of common ground between the groups. Teaching centers in the new normal would be the garage—not places for faculty to be repaired, but "garages" in the spirit of Jobs, Wozniak, and others, who created the first Apple computer—where creative faculty members gather to take risks, innovate, and transform the educational landscape.

We were struck by how closely this vision of the new normal meshes with our descriptions of faculty development practices, priorities, and imperatives emerging from this study and represented by the maturing Age of the Network and the emerging Age of Evidence. As we move into the next decade, how do faculty developers help to build this new normal? We offer a final set of questions for consideration.

- How do faculty developers help to break down the divisions and hierarchies that often structure teaching and learning on their campuses?
- As faculty development encircles a wider set of partners, how do developers negotiate their roles? When do they lead, when do they collaborate, and when do they follow the lead of others?
- If a heightened purpose in the new normal is to position faculty developers as change agents, how do they continue to be perceived as champions of the faculty, and not as the handmaids of the administration?
- What should be the role of centers for teaching and learning in working with others—at individual, department, and institutional levels—to define outstanding teaching quality and measure it? What should be the role of centers in providing evidence of quality teaching?
- How do centers respond to current questions about the validity and reliability of student ratings, peer review, and self-reflection and the difficulties in calibrating the combination of instructor and student contributions in the assessment of teaching and learning?
- How do developers make the evaluation of teaching authentic and provide feedback that instructors are open to?

For the POD Network and the growing number of other professional associations that may include faculty development in their focus, we close by asking the following:

- What kind of organizational priorities will be most important as developers work in a highly networked and evidence-based environment, locally, nationally, and globally?
- What mission priorities, membership portfolios, networking and

mentoring opportunities, conferences, and publications will be most useful to members in building their capacities to meet the challenges that the next decade of change in higher education will bring?

These and the other questions posed throughout this chapter point to this maturing Age of the Network as setting the foundation for increasing the centrality and relevance of faculty development in higher education institutions and the emerging Age of Evidence as rich in possibilities for developers to take greater leadership roles in shaping the ways teaching, learning, and faculty work are conceptualized, defined, enacted, supported, evaluated, and improved. We believe that the field of faculty development has an exciting future ahead, and we look forward to joining our colleagues nationally and internationally in exploring how we answer these questions and shape faculty development in the ages to come.

Survey Instrument

1. This question was reserved in the online version for consent language and agreement.

2. Please indicate any of the following titles or roles that apply to you.

   - Director
   - Program Coordinator
   - Senior-Level Administrator
   - Faculty Member
   - Associate/Assistant Director
   - Technology Consultant/Designer/Coordinator
   - Instructional Consultant/Designer/Coordinator
   - Other, please specify

3. What is your primary title or role?

   - Director
   - Program Coordinator
   - Senior-Level Administrator
   - Faculty Member
   - Associate/Assistant Director
   - Technology Consultant/Designer/Coordinator
   - Instructional Consultant/Designer/Coordinator
   - Other, please specify

4. If you indicated that you are a faculty member, please indicate your field of study.

5. What position did you hold immediately prior to your current position?

   - Director
   - Program Coordinator
   - Senior-Level Administrator
   - Faculty Member
   - Associate/Assistant Director
   - Technology Consultant/Designer/Coordinator
   - Instructional Consultant/Designer/Coordinator
   - Other, please specify

6. How long have you held a position of responsibility in faculty development?

Years Total _____
Years at This Institution _____

7. What is your gender?

- Female
- Male
- Prefer not to answer

8. Please specify your race.

- American Indian or Alaska Native
- Asian
- Black or African American
- Native Hawaiian or Pacific Islander
- White/Caucasian
- Other, please specify
- Prefer not to answer

9. Please choose the age range inclusive of your current age.

- 24 or younger
- 25–29
- 30–34
- 35–39
- 40–44
- 45–49
- 50–54
- 55–59
- 60–64
- 65 or older
- Prefer not to answer

10. What is your highest completed level of education?

- Associate Degree
- Undergraduate/Bachelor's Degree
- Master's Degree

- Doctoral/Terminal Degree
- Other, please specify

11. Please specify the discipline/field of your highest degree.

12. Which of these classifications most accurately describes your institution?

- Associate College/Community College/Technical School
- Baccalaureate/Bachelor's College or University
- Master's College or University
- Doctorate-Granting University
- Special Focus Institution (e.g., medical school)
- Tribal College
- Other, please specify

13. Is your institution

- Private, for profit
- Private, nonprofit
- Public

14. In what country is your institution located?

- United States
- Canada
- Other, please specify

15. Please indicate which of the following best describes your institution.

- Historically Black College or University (HBCU)
- Minority-Serving College or University
- Other, please specify
- None of these applies to my institution

Questions 16–33 were administered only to those who indicated they were directors.

16. What best describes your institution's faculty development structure?

- A "clearinghouse" for programs and offerings that are sponsored across the institution, but offering few programs itself

- A committee charged with supporting faculty development
- An individual faculty member or administrator charged with supporting faculty development
- A single centralized unit with dedicated staff
- Structures such as a system-wide office
- Other, please specify

17. How long has the faculty development office or department on your campus had this structure?

- 0–11 months
- 12 months–2 years
- 3–5 years
- 6–10 years
- 11–20 years
- If longer than 20 years, please specify

18. How many FTE [full-time equivalent] staff do you have in the structure you indicated previously in the following categories?
- Director
- Assistant/Associate Director
- Academic/Professional/Consulting Staff
- Support or Secretarial Staff
- Graduate Students
- Undergraduate Students
- Other, please specify

19. To whom do you report?

- President
- Provost
- Associate/Assistant/Vice Provost
- Dean/Associate Dean
- Vice President/Vice-Chancellor
- Other, please specify

20. What is your annual operating budget minus staff salaries, external grants, onetime funds, or "carry over" (e.g., your programming budget)?

- $0–$24,999 USD
- $25,000–$49,999 USD

- $50,000–$99,999 USD
- $100,000–$149,999 USD
- $150,000–$199,999 USD
- $200,000–$249,999 USD
- $250,000–$299,999 USD
- $300,000–$399,999 USD
- $400,000–$499,999 USD
- $500,000 USD or more

21. Please indicate all of the additional sources from which your office has received funding beyond your annual operating budget within the past three years:

- External grants
- Endowment/gift funds
- Carry-over funds
- Onetime university allocations for special projects
- Cost-share with other units
- None
- Other, please specify

22. If you have had funds that augment your base programming budget, please let us know how much they are and what they are used for.

23. Program Goals and Purposes: Faculty development programs may be guided by various goals and purposes. From the following list of possibilities, please indicate the degree to which your program/unit is guided by any of the following purposes:

NS—Not Sure
1—Not at all
2—To a slight extent
3—To a moderate extent
4—To a great extent

a. To act as a change agent within the institution
b. To advance new initiatives in teaching and learning
c. To create or sustain a culture of teaching excellence
d. To foster collegiality within and among faculty members and/or departments
e. To help the institution respond to accreditation, quality enhancement plans

f. To partner in the learning enterprise with libraries, technology centers, research offices, and so on.

g. To position the institution at the forefront of educational innovation

h. To provide recognition and reward for excellence in teaching

i. To provide support for faculty members who are experiencing difficulties with their teaching

j. To respond to and support individual faculty members' goals for professional development

k. To respond to critical needs as defined by the institution

l. To support departmental goals, planning, and development

m. Other

24. If you rated "Other" in the previous question, please specify here what additional guiding goal or purpose you rated. You may also use this space for additional comments on your ratings.

25. Please indicate the three primary purposes that guide your program, using the list in question 23.

- To act as a change agent within the institution
- To advance new initiatives in teaching and learning
- To create or sustain a culture of teaching excellence
- To foster collegiality within and among faculty members and/or departments
- To help the institution respond to accreditation, quality enhancement plans
- To partner in the learning enterprise with libraries, technology centers, research offices, and so on.
- To position the institution at the forefront of educational innovation
- To provide recognition and reward for excellence in teaching
- To provide support for faculty members who are experiencing difficulties with their teaching
- To respond to and support individual faculty members' goals for professional development
- To respond to critical needs as defined by the institution
- To support departmental goals, planning, and development
- Other

26. What other units or individuals at your institution offer faculty development programming?

NS—Not Sure
1—Not at all
2—To a slight extent
3—To a moderate extent
4—To a great extent

- Assessment Offices
- Campus Sustainability Offices
- Community/Service-Learning–Directors/Centers
- Deans/Assistant/Associate Deans (e.g., within individual colleges)
- Federal, State, or Foundation Grant Programs
- International Affairs/Study Abroad
- Graduate College
- Teaching Assistant (TA) Support and Development Programs
- Honors College
- Libraries
- Offices of Diversity/Inclusion
- Research Affairs
- Student Affairs and Residence Life
- Technology Centers
- Writing Centers
- Other

27. If you rated "Other" in the previous question, please indicate which other units or individuals you rated. You may include additional comments on your ratings.

28. To what extent do you collaborate with other units or individuals at your institution who offer faculty development programming?

NS—Not Sure
1—Not at all
2—To a slight extent
3—To a moderate extent
4—To a great extent

- Assessment Offices
- Campus Sustainability Offices
- Community/Service-Learning Directors/Centers
- Deans/Assistant/Associate Deans (e.g., within individual colleges)
- Federal, State, or Foundation Grant Programs

- International Affairs/Study Abroad
- Graduate College
- Teaching Assistant (TA) Support and Development Programs
- Honors College
- Libraries
- Offices of Diversity/Inclusion
- Research Affairs
- Student Affairs and Residence Life
- Technology Centers
- Writing Centers
- Other

29. If you rated "Other" in the previous question, please indicate which other units or individuals you rated. You may also include additional comments on your ratings.

30. To what extent do you collect data on the following kinds of impact of your practices?

    NS—Not Sure
    1—Not at all
    2—To a slight extent
    3—To a moderate extent
    4—To a great extent

- Numbers served through your programs
- Satisfaction of participants
- Increase in the knowledge or skills of the participants
- Change in the practice of participants
- Change in the learning or behavior of those served by the participants
- Change in the institution
- Other

31. If you rated "Other" in the previous question, please specify the impacts/outcomes you measure here. You may also include additional comments on your ratings.

32. For each, how do you college the data. Please choose all that apply.

	Participation tracking and record collection	Participant Self-Report Surveys	Interviews	Observation	Collection of student assignments, projects, exam scores	Planned research projects that assess change	Tracking of development and dissemination of SoTL projects by faculty
Numbers served through your programs							
Satisfaction of participants							
Increase in the knowledge or skills of the participants							
Change in the practice of participants							
Change in the learning or behavior of those served by the participants							
Change in the institution							

33. Which of the following methods do you use to disseminate the results of your impact assessments? Please choose all that apply.

- Report to advisory board
- Publication in annual report
- Presentation of data on the institution's website
- Presentation at conferences or meetings external to your campus
- Publication in journals, book chapters, or other broadly disseminated outlets
- Other, please specify

34. Overall, what is the target audience for your services? Please choose all that apply.

- Tenure-Track Faculty
- Fixed-Term Faculty
- Part-Time/Adjunct Faculty

- Graduate Students
- Academic Staff
- Other, please specify

35. Teaching and Learning: Please indicate the extent to which your faculty development program is currently offering services pertaining to each of the following issues.

NS—Not Sure
1—Not at all
2—To a slight extent
3—To a moderate extent
4—To a great extent

1. Active, inquiry-based, or problem-based learning
2. Multiculturalism and diversity related to teaching
3. Teaching underprepared students
4. Teaching adult learners
5. Integrating technology into "traditional" teaching and learning settings (e.g., clickers)
7. Teaching in online and distance environments*
8. Blended learning approaches
9. Team teaching
10. Community service-learning
11. Writing across the curriculum/writing to learn
12. Sustainability across the curriculum
13. Peer review of teaching
14. Scholarship of teaching and learning (SoTL)
15. Creating course/teaching portfolios

*Number 7 is correct; an error in numbering existed within the survey.

36. Faculty Work and Career Development: Please indicate the extent to which your faculty development program is currently offering services pertaining to each of the following issues.

NS—Not Sure
1—Not at all
2—To a slight extent
3—To a moderate extent

4—To a great extent

16. Ethical conduct of faculty work
17. New faculty orientation/development
18. Midcareer and senior faculty development
19. International faculty development
20. Mentoring programs
21. Teaching assistant development
22. Preparing the future professoriate (e.g., preparing future faculty, CIRTL)
23. Tenure and promotion preparation
24. Post-tenure review
25. Time management in faculty work
26. Work-life balance
27. Orientation and support for part-time/adjunct faculty
28. Orientation and support for fixed-term faculty
29. Sabbatical planning
30. Scholarly writing
31. Leadership development for faculty

37. Educational/Institutional Improvement: Please indicate the extent to which your faculty development program is currently offering services pertaining to each of the following issues.

NS—Not Sure
1—Not at all
2—To a slight extent
3—To a moderate extent
4—To a great extent

32. Assessment of student learning outcomes
33. Course and curriculum reform
34. General education reform
35. Program assessment (e.g., for accreditation)
36. Unit/program evaluation
37. Departmental leadership and management
38. Faculty and departmental entrepreneurship (e.g., consulting on behalf of the institution)
39. Interdisciplinary collaborations
40. Other

38. If you rated "Other" in the previous question, please identify it here. You may also use this space for additional comments on your ratings.

39. Of the services offered in response to the issues listed in items 1 through 40, which three do you consider your "signature services"?

40. What three services in response to issues listed in items 1 through 40 would you add or expand in your portfolio if you were given the opportunity/additional resources?

41. From items 1 through 40, what do you think are the top three issues that faculty development should address over the next five years?

42. Faculty Development Program Approaches: Please indicate the extent to which your faculty development program is currently offering services using each of the following approaches.

NS—Not Sure
1—Not at all
2—To a slight extent
3—To a moderate extent
4—To a great extent

1. Individual consultation
2. Teaching observation and feedback with a trained consultant
3. Peer observation of teaching with feedback
4. Small-Group Instructional Diagnosis (SGID)
5. Informal discussions with colleagues about teaching problems and solutions over coffee or lunch
6. Department/discipline-specific workshops (on demand)
7. Hands-on workshops (1–3 hours)
8. Institutes/retreats (2–3 full days)
9. Seminars (multiple-meeting commitment)
10. Structured discussions focused around a reading provided prior to the meeting (e.g., Journal Club)
11. Faculty and professional learning communities (i.e., full semester or academic year, regular meetings)
12. Web-based resources (e.g., links to articles or Internet content)
13. Webinars (1- to 2-hour synchronous Web-based seminars that can be saved and viewed later)
14. Asynchronous online programs
15. Electronic newsletter
16. Other

43. If you rated "Other" in the preceding question, please indicate here what additional approach is being used by your faculty development program. You may also include additional comments on your ratings.

44. Of the approaches that you indicated are being used by your institution in items 1 through 16, which three do you consider your "signature" approaches?

45. What three approaches in response to the issues listed in items 1 through 16 would you add or expand in your portfolio if you were given the opportunity and/or additional resources?

46. From the items in question 42, what do you think are the top three approaches on which faculty development should focus over the next 5 years?

47. In what directions do you think the field of faculty development *should* move in the next decade?

48. In what directions do you think the field of faculty development *will* move in the next decade?

49. Please feel free to comment on this survey or write about any other thoughts that occurred to you while completing it.

Services Tables by Institution Type

TABLE B.1

Extent to Which Services Pertaining to Teaching and Learning Are Offered

Services	N	All Mean (SD)	R/D Mean (SD)	Comp Mean (SD)	LA Mean (SD)	CC Mean (SD)	Can Mean (SD)
Integrating technology into traditional teaching and learning settings (e.g., clickers)	330	3.28 (.85)	3.26 (.84)	3.28 (.88)	3.39 (.90)	3.13 (.90)	3.41 (.84)
Active, inquiry-based, or problem-based learning	322	3.25 (.88)	3.29 (.89)	3.08 (1.01)	3.28 (.77)	3.20 (.93)	3.41 (.84)
Blended learning approaches	321	2.88 (1.02)	2.93 (1.05)	2.71 (1.04)	2.97 (.98)	2.83 (1.04)	3.07 (1.00)
Teaching in online and distance environments	326	2.83 (1.10)	2.86 (1.11)	2.69 (1.03)	2.81 (1.09)	2.70 (1.18)	3.08 (1.13)
Scholarship of teaching and learning (SoTL)	320	2.80 (1.03)	2.77 (1.00)	2.75 (1.00)	2.77 (1.28)	2.66 (1.01)	3.04 (1.04)
Multiculturalism and diversity related to teaching	326	2.60 (.99)	2.75 (1.00)	2.48 (1.05)	2.52 (.91)	2.23 (.77)	2.85 (.864)
Creating course/teaching portfolios	314	2.50 (1.09)	2.47 (1.08)	2.46 (1.09)	2.65 (1.08)	2.52 (1.15)	2.68 (.95)
Teaching underprepared students	326	2.42 (1.01)	2.43 (1.01)	2.36 (1.08)	2.53 (.88)	2.27 (.98)	2.44 (.89)
Community service-learning	317	2.37 (.98)	2.37 (.97)	2.12 (1.05)	2.58 (1.03)	2.38 (.94)	2.77 (.86)
Writing across the curriculum/writing to learn	320	2.35 (1.02)	2.39 (1.03)	2.32 (1.04)	2.47 (1.01)	1.83 (.89)	2.58 (.99)
Peer review of teaching	322	2.35 (.98)	2.37 (1.02)	2.29 (1.00)	2.35 (1.02)	2.21 (.90)	2.56 (.89)
Teaching adult learners	320	2.26 (1.04)	2.24 (1.06)	2.07 (.99)	2.19 (1.06)	2.19 (1.11)	2.54 (.91)
Team teaching	307	1.94 (.86)	1.97 (.88)	1.79 (.83)	1.93 (.77)	1.93 (.87)	2.31 (.93)
Sustainability across the curriculum	308	1.83 (.93)	1.82 (.94)	1.83 (.94)	1.42 (.58)	1.76 (.87)	2.08 (.98)

Note. R/D = research/doctoral institutions; Comp = comprehensive institutions; LA = liberal arts colleges; CC = community colleges; Can = Canadian institutions.

TABLE B.2

Extent to Which Services Pertaining to Faculty Work and Career Development Are Offered

Services	N	All Mean (SD)	R/D Mean (SD)	Comp Mean (SD)	LA Mean (SD)	CC Mean (SD)	Can Mean (SD)
New faculty orientation/ development	328	3.48 (.78)	3.41 (.80)	3.43 (.83)	3.55 (.79)	3.77 (.57)	3.63 (.63)
Mentoring programs	309	2.71 (.80)	2.69 (.81)	2.51 (.72)	2.80 (.81)	2.87 (.73)	2.93 (.87)
Orientation and support for part-time/adjunct faculty	317	2.62 (1.05)	2.67 (1.04)	2.78 (1.05)	2.63 (1.10)	2.57 (1.01)	2.17 (.92)
Orientation and support for fixed-term faculty	299	2.61 (1.10)	2.65 (1.04)	2.62 (1.15)	2.54 (1.29)	2.43 (1.10)	2.56 (1.04)
Midcareer and senior faculty development	318	2.59 (.98)	2.63 (.97)	2.50 (.93)	2.61 (1.15)	2.57 (.94)	2.62 (.94)
Tenure and promotion preparation	306	2.32 (1.10)	2.45 (1.06)	2.07 (1.08)	2.41 (1.15)	2.07 (1.10)	2.48 (1.16)
Teaching assistant development	290	2.21 (1.31)	2.11 (1.26)	2.43 (1.27)	2.19 (1.39)	2.13 (1.39)	2.48 (1.42)
Scholarly writing	305	2.03 (1.06)	2.04 (1.05)	1.88 (.97)	2.11 (1.10)	2.03 (1.15)	2.19 (1.18)
Leadership development for faculty	313	2.00 (.99)	2.01 (.93)	1.81 (.91)	1.97 (1.09)	2.00 (1.08)	2.35 (1.16)
Preparing the future professoriate (e.g., PFF, CIRTL)	281	1.99 (1.24)	1.96 (1.24)	2.06 (1.20)	2.07 (1.24)	1.88 (1.19)	1.92 (1.32)
Work-life balance	311	1.95 (.88)	1.94 (.86)	1.91 (.83)	1.93 (.92)	1.97 (1.02)	2.08 (.93)
Time management in faculty work	307	1.94 (.83)	1.96 (.82)	1.95 (.82)	1.97 (.82)	1.80 (.85)	2.00 (.83)
International faculty development	297	1.80 (.91)	1.81 (.93)	1.67 (.82)	2.10 (.92)	1.66 (.90)	1.80 (1.00)
Ethical conduct of faculty work	301	1.71 (.90)	1.70 (.86)	1.59 (.86)	1.83 (1.02)	1.60 (.93)	1.65 (.83)
Posttenure review	294	1.59 (.89)	1.62 (.87)	1.30 (.66)	2.00 (1.12)	1.32 (.61)	1.78 (1.09)
Sabbatical planning	293	1.46 (.87)	1.47 (.89)	1.56 (.94)	1.48 (.94)	1.30 (.72)	1.33 (.76)

Note. R/D = research/doctoral institutions; Comp = comprehensive institutions; LA = liberal arts colleges; CC = community colleges; Can = Canadian institutions; PFF = preparing future faculty; CIRTL = Center for the Integration of Research, Teaching, and Learning.

TABLE B.3

Extent to Which Services Pertaining to Educational/Institutional Improvement Are Offered

Services	N	All Mean (SD)	R/D Mean (SD)	Comp Mean (SD)	LA Mean (SD)	CC Mean (SD)	Can Mean (SD)
Assessment of student learning outcomes	329	3.21 (.87)	3.15 (.92)	3.23 (.85)	3.36 (.74)	3.23 (.86)	3.22 (.93)
Course and curriculum reform	324	3.08 (.95)	3.03 (.96)	3.08 (.93)	3.25 (.80)	3.00 (.98)	2.96 (1.15)
Other services	81	2.63 (1.29)	2.60 (1.19)	3.14 (1.46)	3.10 (1.29)	1.57 (1.13)	2.90 (1.37)
Program assessment (e.g., for accreditation)	321	2.61 (1.10)	2.58 (1.16)	2.72 (1.04)	2.61 (.92)	2.69 (.104)	2.28 (1.17)
General education reform	313	2.48 (1.07)	2.43 (1.06)	2.54 (1.14)	2.43 (.94)	2.72 (.92)	2.16 (1.21)
Interdisciplinary collaborations	318	2.34 (1.00)	2.29 (.94)	2.33 (1.06)	2.48 (1.09)	2.43 (1.17)	2.28 (.98)
Unit/program evaluation	312	2.22 (1.05)	2.14 (1.07)	2.21 (.94)	2.32 (1.08)	2.32 (1.06)	1.96 (.98)
Departmental leadership and management	315	1.92 (.99)	1.86 (.97)	1.78 (.91)	1.93 (1.08)	2.00 (1.00)	2.35 (.98)
Faculty and departmental entrepreneurship (e.g., consulting on behalf of the institution)	290	1.38 (.71)	1.35 (.67)	1.34 (.68)	1.68 (.91)	1.33 (.62)	1.36 (.79)

Note. R/D = research/doctoral institutions; Comp = comprehensive institutions; LA = liberal arts colleges; CC = community colleges; Can = Canadian institutions.

TABLE B.4

Developers' Choices for Top Three Signature Services

Services	All	R/D	Comp	LA	CC	Can
N	298	136	58	36	27	23
New faculty orientation/development	37%	35%	35%	40%	41%	39%
Active, inquiry-based, or problem-based learning	35%	40%	24%	23%	37%	52%
Integrating technology into traditional teaching and learning settings (e.g., clickers)	24%	24%	21%	17%	37%	26%
Course and curriculum reform	20%	22%	17%	27%	11%	4%
Assessment of student learning outcomes	17%	24%	10%	13%	15%	4%
Teaching in online and distance environments	16%	1%	19%	20%	11%	17%
Scholarship of teaching and learning (SoTL)	15%	17%	14%	7%	7%	30%
Teaching assistant development	11%	8%	17%	13%	7%	17%
Blended learning approaches	8%	15%	21%	7%	0%	0%
Preparing the future professoriate (e.g., PFF, CIRTL)	8%	8%	9%	7%	7%	13%
Mentoring programs	8%	7%	3%	3%	22%	13%
Teaching adult learners	7%	7%	9%	7%	7%	9%
Orientation and support for part-time/adjunct faculty	7%	5%	10%	13%	4%	4%
Multiculturalism and diversity related to teaching	6%	7%	2%	7%	11%	4%
Teaching underprepared students	6%	5%	5%	7%	4%	13%
Midcareer and senior faculty development	6%	7%	10%	7%	4%	0%
Tenure and promotion preparation	6%	7%	10%	3%	4%	4%
Program assessment (e.g., for accreditation)	6%	8%	7%	7%	4%	0%
Other issue	5%	4%	3%	13%	4%	13%
Peer review of teaching	5%	4%	7%	7%	4%	0%
General education reform	5%	5%	3%	0%	4%	4%
Creating course/teaching portfolios	4%	3%	9%	0%	4%	4%
Scholarly writing	4%	3%	2%	13%	7%	0%
Leadership development for faculty	4%	4%	3%	3%	4%	0%
Writing across the curriculum/writing to learn	3%	3%	7%	3%	4%	0%
Interdisciplinary collaborations	3%	2%	3%	3%	15%	0%

TABLE B.4 *(Continued)*

Services	All	R/D	Comp	LA	CC	Can
Departmental leadership and management	3%	2%	2%	7%	4%	4%
Community service-learning	3%	4%	2%	3%	0%	0%
International faculty development	2%	2%	2%	3%	0%	0%
Unit/program evaluation	2%	1%	2%	3%	4%	0%
Ethical conduct of faculty work	1%	2%	2%	0%	0%	0%
Orientation and support for fixed-term faculty	1%	1%	3%	0%	0%	0%
Work-life balance	1%	1%	2%	0%	0%	4%
Faculty and departmental entrepreneurship (e.g., consulting on behalf of the institution)	1%	0%	0%	3%	0%	4%
Team teaching	1%	6%	2%	0%	4%	0%
Sustainability across the curriculum	1%	0%	0%	3%	4%	0%
Posttenure review	0%	0%	2%	0%	0%	0%
Time management in faculty work	0%	0%	0%	0%	0%	0%
Sabbatical planning	0%	0%	0%	0%	0%	0%

Note. R/D = research/doctoral institutions; Comp = comprehensive institutions; LA = liberal arts colleges; CC = community colleges; Can = Canadian institutions; PFF = preparing future faculty; CIRTL = Center for the Integration of Research, Teaching, and Learning.

TABLE B.5
Top Services Developers Would Add or Expand

Services	All	R/D	Comp	LA	CC	Can
N	284	133	55	29	26	20
Scholarship of teaching and learning (SoTL)	19%	21%	22%	34%	8%	5%
Midcareer and senior faculty development	19%	21%	18%	21%	15%	25%
Mentoring programs	18%	18%	18%	7%	38%	15%
Multiculturalism and diversity related to teaching	15%	15%	15%	14%	19%	15%
Orientation and support for part-time/adjunct faculty	14%	12%	20%	3%	15%	30%
Departmental leadership and management	14%	17%	9%	7%	19%	15%
Peer review of teaching	13%	13%	13%	10%	15%	25%
Leadership development for faculty	12%	14%	13%	7%	12%	15%
Assessment of student learning outcomes	12%	11%	15%	14%	4%	15%
Teaching underprepared students	11%	13%	13%	17%	0%	5%
Scholarly writing	11%	8%	7%	17%	8%	15%
Active, inquiry-based, or problem-based learning	10%	11%	9%	14%	8%	0%
Interdisciplinary collaborations	10%	8%	7%	21%	8%	10%
Integrating technology into traditional teaching and learning settings (e.g., clickers)	9%	14%	7%	3%	4%	5%
Course and curriculum reform	9%	6%	9%	17%	12%	10%
Teaching in online and distance environments	8%	12%	5%	7%	8%	0%
Blended learning approaches	7%	3%	9%	0%	15%	20%
New faculty orientation/development	7%	4%	13%	0%	15%	5%
Creating course/teaching portfolios	6%	5%	4%	7%	4%	15%
Community service-learning	5%	7%	2%	3%	4%	0%
Teaching assistant development	5%	3%	7%	3%	0%	10%
Tenure and promotion preparation	5%	3%	2%	10%	8%	0%
Work-life balance	5%	6%	4%	10%	0%	5%
General education reform	5%	2%	5%	10%	4%	10%
Program assessment (e.g., for accreditation)	5%	6%	5%	0%	8%	0%
Writing across the curriculum/writing to learn	4%	3%	4%	7%	0%	0%

TABLE B.5 *(Continued)*

Services	All	R/D	Comp	LA	CC	Can
Teaching adult learners	4%	3%	5%	3%	4%	5%
Time management in faculty work	4%	7%	2%	3%	0%	5%
Faculty and departmental entrepreneurship (e.g., consulting on behalf of the institution)	4%	5%	2%	0%	4%	0%
International faculty development	3%	3%	5%	7%	0%	0%
Team teaching	2%	4%	2%	0%	4%	0%
Sustainability across the curriculum	2%	2%	4%	0%	0%	5%
Ethical conduct of faculty work	2%	3%	4%	3%	0%	0%
Preparing the future professoriate (e.g., PFF, CIRTL)	2%	2%	2%	3%	4%	0%
Posttenure review	2%	2%	2%	0%	0%	0%
Sabbatical planning	2%	2%	2%	0%	4%	0%
Unit/program evaluation	2%	2%	4%	3%	8%	0%
Orientation and support for fixed-term faculty	1%	2%	0%	0%	0%	0%
Other issue	1%	1%	0%	3%	0%	0%

Note. R/D = research/doctoral institutions; Comp = comprehensive institutions; LA = liberal arts colleges; CC = community colleges; Can = Canadian institutions; PFF = preparing future faculty; CIRTL = Center for the Integration of Research, Teaching, and Learning.

TABLE B.6
Top Services Faculty Development Should Address Over the Next Five Years

Services	All	R/D	Comp	LA	CC	Can
N	385	174	69	38	35	33
Assessment of student learning outcomes	18%	21%	25%	13%	17%	9%
Teaching in online and distance environments	16%	21%	10%	13%	9%	12%
Blended learning approaches	14%	12%	19%	11%	11%	12%
Active, inquiry-based, or problem-based learning	13%	11%	15%	18%	17%	18%
Multiculturalism and diversity related to teaching	13%	12%	9%	16%	23%	15%
Teaching underprepared students	13%	15%	9%	11%	6%	15%
Course and curriculum reform	12%	9%	19%	11%	23%	3%
Leadership development for faculty	12%	11%	19%	18%	11%	3%
Interdisciplinary collaborations	9%	11%	9%	8%	17%	0%
Integrating technology into traditional teaching and learning settings (e.g., clickers)	9%	8%	13%	3%	9%	6%
Midcareer and senior faculty development	8%	8%	7%	11%	6%	9%
Departmental leadership and management	8%	11%	4%	0%	11%	6%
Scholarship of teaching and learning (SoTL)	7%	9%	7%	11%	0%	6%
Work-life balance	7%	9%	3%	5%	3%	9%
Mentoring programs	6%	8%	9%	3%	3%	0%
Peer review of teaching	4%	4%	6%	3%	6%	3%
Program assessment (e.g., for accreditation)	4%	6%	4%	3%	3%	3%
Orientation and support for part-time/adjunct faculty	4%	5%	1%	5%	9%	3%
General education reform	4%	4%	3%	0%	0%	6%
International faculty development	4%	2%	4%	13%	6%	3%
New faculty orientation/development	4%	2%	9%	0%	6%	3%
Sustainability across the curriculum	3%	3%	0%	5%	3%	3%
Teaching adult learners	2%	2%	9%	0%	6%	0%
Preparing the future professoriate (e.g., PFF, CIRTL)	2%	3%	1%	5%	0%	0%
Teaching assistant development	2%	0%	6%	8%	0%	0%
Unit/program evaluation	2%	1%	4%	5%	3%	3%

TABLE B.6 *(Continued)*

Services	All	R/D	Comp	LA	CC	Can
Faculty and departmental entrepreneurship (e.g., consulting on behalf of the institution)	2%	2%	1%	8%	0%	3%
Writing across the curriculum/writing to learn	2%	1%	6%	0%	0%	0%
Time management in faculty work	2%	2%	1%	0%	6%	0%
Ethical conduct of faculty work	2%	2%	3%	0%	0%	0%
Other issue	2%	1%	1%	5%	0%	6%
Community service-learning	1%	2%	0%	0%	0%	0%
Creating course/teaching portfolios	1%	2%	1%	3%	0%	0%
Tenure and promotion preparation	1%	1%	0%	3%	0%	3%
Scholarly writing	1%	0%	1%	3%	0%	6%
Team teaching	1%	1%	0%	0%	0%	3%
Orientation and support for fixed-term faculty	1%	1%	0%	0%	0%	0%
Posttenure review	1%	1%	1%	0%	0%	0%
Sabbatical planning	0%	0%	0%	0%	0%	0%

Note. R/D = research/doctoral institutions; Comp = comprehensive institutions; LA = liberal arts colleges; CC = community colleges; Can = Canadian institutions; PFF = preparing future faculty; CIRTL = Center for the Integration of Research, Teaching, and Learning.

Top Issues Faculty Development Should Address in the Next Five Years

TABLE C.1

Top Issues Faculty Development Should Address in the Next Five Years by Institutional Type

Issues	All	R/D	Comp	LA	CC	Can
N	385	174	69	38	35	33
Assessment of student learning outcomes	18%	21%	25%	13%	17%	9%
Teaching in online and distance environments	16%	21%	10%	13%	9%	12%
Blended learning approaches	14%	12%	19%	11%	11%	12%
Active, inquiry-based, or problem-based learning	13%	11%	15%	18%	17%	18%
Multiculturalism and diversity related to teaching	13%	12%	9%	16%	23%	15%
Teaching underprepared students	13%	15%	9%	11%	6%	15%
Course and curriculum reform	12%	9%	19%	11%	23%	3%
Leadership development for faculty	12%	11%	19%	18%	11%	3%
Interdisciplinary collaborations	9%	11%	9%	8%	17%	0%
Integrating technology into traditional teaching and learning settings (e.g., clickers)	9%	8%	13%	3%	9%	6%
Midcareer and senior faculty development	8%	8%	7%	11%	6%	9%
Departmental leadership and management	8%	11%	4%	0%	11%	6%
Scholarship of teaching and learning (SoTL)	7%	9%	7%	11%	0%	6%
Work-life balance	7%	9%	3%	5%	3%	9%
Mentoring programs	6%	8%	9%	3%	3%	0%
Peer review of teaching	4%	4%	6%	3%	6%	3%
Program assessment (e.g., for accreditation)	4%	6%	4%	3%	3%	3%
Orientation and support for part-time/adjunct faculty	4%	5%	1%	5%	9%	3%
General education reform	4%	4%	3%	0%	0%	6%
International faculty development	4%	2%	4%	13%	6%	3%
New faculty orientation/development	4%	2%	9%	0%	6%	3%
Sustainability across the curriculum	3%	3%	0%	5%	3%	3%

(Continues)

TABLE C.1 *(Continued)*

Issues	All	R/D	Comp	LA	CC	Can
Teaching adult learners	2%	2%	9%	0%	6%	0%
Preparing the future professoriate (e.g., PFF, CIRTL)	2%	3%	1%	5%	0%	0%
Teaching assistant development	2%	0%	6%	8%	0%	0%
Unit/program evaluation	2%	1%	4%	5%	3%	3%
Faculty and departmental entrepreneurship (e.g., consulting on behalf of the institution)	2%	2%	1%	8%	0%	3%
Writing across the curriculum/writing to learn	2%	1%	6%	0%	0%	0%
Time management in faculty work	2%	2%	1%	0%	6%	0%
Ethical conduct of faculty work	2%	2%	3%	0%	0%	0%
Other issue	2%	1%	1%	5%	0%	6%
Community service-learning	1%	2%	0%	0%	0%	0%
Creating course/teaching portfolios	1%	2%	1%	3%	0%	0%
Tenure and promotion preparation	1%	1%	0%	3%	0%	3%
Scholarly writing	1%	0%	1%	3%	0%	6%
Team teaching	1%	1%	0%	0%	0%	3%
Orientation and support for fixed-term faculty	1%	1%	0%	0%	0%	0%
Posttenure review	1%	1%	1%	0%	0%	0%
Sabbatical planning	0%	0%	0%	0%	0%	0%

Note. R/D = research/doctoral institutions; Comp = comprehensive institutions; LA = liberal arts colleges; CC = community colleges; Can = Canadian institutions; PFF = preparing future faculty; CIRTL = Center for the Integration of Research, Teaching, and Learning.

REFERENCES

Adams, M., & Bell, L. A. (Eds.). (2016). *Teaching for diversity and social justice*. New York, NY: Routledge.

Ambrose, S. A., Bridges, M. W., DiPietro, M., Lovett, M. C., & Norman, M. K. (2010). *How learning works: Seven research-based principles for smart teaching*. San Francisco, CA: Jossey-Bass.

American Association for the Advancement of Science. (2011). *Vision and change in undergraduate biology education: A callege to action*. Washington, DC: Author.

Austin, A. E., Sorcinelli, M. D., & McDaniels, M. (2007). Understanding new faculty background, aspirations, challenges, and growth. In In R. P. Perry & J. C. Smart (Eds.), *The scholarship of teaching and learning in higher education: An evidence-based perspective* (pp. 39–89). Dordrecht, the Netherlands: Springer.

Baldwin, R. G., & Zeig, M. J. (2012). Making emeritus matter. *Change, 44*(5), 28–34.

Baldwin, R. G., & Zeig, M. J. (2013). Emeritus colleges: Enriching academic communities by extending academic life. *Innovative Higher Education, 38*(5), 355–368.

Banks, J. A. (2015). *Cultural diversity and education: Foundation, curriculum and teaching*. New York, NY: Routledge.

Barr, R. B., & Tagg, J. (1995). From teaching to learning: A new paradigm for undergraduate education. *Change, 27*(6), 13–25.

Beach, A. L. (2015). Boyer's impact on faculty development. In D. Moser, T. C. Ream, & J. M. Braxton (Eds.), *25th anniversary edition: Scholarship reconsidered* (pp. 13–18). San Francisco, CA: Jossey-Bass.

Beach, A. L., & Cox, M. D. (2009). The impact of faculty learning communities on teaching and learning. *Learning Communities Journal, 1*(1), 7–27.

Beach, A. L., Henderson, C., & Finkelstein, N. (2012). Facilitating change in undergraduate STEM education. *Change, 44*(6), 52–59.

Bell, A., & Mladenovic, R. (2008). The benefits of peer observation of teaching for tutor development. *Higher Education, 55*(6), 735–752.

Bergquist, W. H., & Phillips, S. R. (1975). Components of an effective faculty development program. *Journal of Higher Education, 46*(2), 177–215.

Beyer, C. H., Taylor, E., & Gillmore, G. M. (2013). *Inside the undergraduate teaching experience: The University of Washington's growth in faculty teaching study*. Albany, NY: SUNY Press.

Bierwert, C. (2012). Strengthening diversity through faculty development. In C. Cook & M. Kaplan (Eds.), *Advancing the culture of teaching on campus: How a teaching center can make a difference* (pp. 137–150). Sterling, VA: Stylus.

Bonner, F. A., II, Marbley, A. F., Tuitt, F., Robinson, P. A., Banda, R. M., & Hughes, R. L. (2014). *Black faculty in the academy: Narratives for negotiating identity and achieving career success.* New York, NY: Routledge.

Bowen, J. A. (2012). *Teaching naked: How moving technology out of your college classroom will improve student learning.* San Francisco, CA: Wiley.

Bowen, W. G. (2013). Higher education in the digital age. *British Journal of Educational Technology, 44*(6), E220–E221.

Bradshaw, J. (2013, September 5). For a new kind of professor, teaching comes first. *Globe and Mail,* 1.

Bryk, A. S., Gomez, L., Grunow, A., & LeMahieu, P. (2015). *Learning to improve: How America's schools can get better at getting better.* Stanford, CA: Carnegie Foundation for the Advancement of Teaching.

Buhl, L. C., & Wilson, L. A. (1984). Foreword. In L. C. Buhl & L. A. Wilson (Eds.), *To improve the academy* (pp. iii–iv). Pittsburg, PA: Duffs Business Institute.

Buller, J. L. (2012). *Best practices in faculty evaluation: A practical guide for academic leaders.* San Francisco, CA: Wiley.

Centra, J. A. (1976). *Faculty development practices in U.S. colleges and universities.* Princeton, NJ: Educational Testing Service.

Chism, N. V. N., Gosling, D., & Sorcinelli, M. D. (2010). International faculty development: Pursuing our work with colleagues around the world. In K. H. Gillespie & D. L. Robertson (Eds.), *A guide to faculty development* (pp. 243–258). San Francisco, CA: Jossey-Bass.

Chism, N. V. N., & Szabo, B. (1998). How faculty development programs evaluate their services. *Journal of Staff, Program & Organization Development, 15*(2), 55–62.

Chism, N. V. N., & Banta, T. W. (2007). Enhancing institutional assessment efforts through qualitative methods. *New Directions for Institutional Research, 136,* 15–28.

Chism, N. V. N., Holley, M., & Harris, C. J. (2012). Researching the impact of educational development: Basis for informed practice. In J. E. Garcia & L. Cruz (Eds.), *To Improve the Academy, Volume 31,* (pp. 129–145). Hoboken, NJ: Wiley.

Coates, T. N. (2015). *Between the world and me.* Melbourne, Australia: Text.

Cohen, P. A., & McKeachie, W. J. (1980). The role of colleagues in the evaluation of college teaching. *Improving College and University Teaching, 28*(4), 147–154.

Condon, W., Iverson, E. R., Manduca, C. A., Rutz, C., & Willett, G. (2016). *Faculty development and student learning: Assessing the connections.* Bloomington, IN: Indiana University Press.

Cook, C., & Kaplan, M. (2011). *Advancing the culture of teaching on campus: How a teaching center can make a difference.* Sterling, VA: Stylus.

Cox, M. D. (2004). Introduction to faculty learning communities. *New Directions for Teaching and Learning, 97,* 5–23.

Debowski, S. (2011). Emergent shifts in faculty development: A reflective review. In J. M. Miller & J. Groccia (Eds.), *To improve the academy: Resources for faculty, instructional, and organizational development* (pp. 306–322). San Francisco, CA: Jossey-Bass.

Dezure, D., Van Note Chism, N., Sorcinelli, M. D., Cheong, G., Ellozy, A. R., Holley, M., . . . Atrushi, D. (2012). Building international faculty development collaborations: The evolving role of American teaching centers. *Change, 44*(3), 24–33.

Eagan, K., Stolzenberg, E. B., Lozano, J. B., Aragon, M. C., Suchard, M. R., & Hurtado, S. (2014). *Undergraduate teaching faculty: The 2013–2014 HERI Faculty Survey.* Los Angeles, CA: Higher Education Research Institute.

Erickson, G. (1986). A survey of faculty development practices. In M. Svinicki, J. Kurfiss, & J. Stone (Eds.), *To improve the academy: Vol. 5. Resources for faculty, instructional, and organizational development* (pp. 182–196). Stillwater, OK: New Forums Press.

Fink, L. D. (2013). *Creating significant learning experiences: An integrated approach to designing college courses.* Hoboken, NJ: Wiley.

Fry, C. L. (Ed.). (2014). *Achieving systemic change: A sourcebook for advancing and funding undergraduate STEM education.* Washington, DC: Association of American Colleges and Universities.

Gaff, J. G. (1975). *Toward faculty renewal: Advances in faculty, instructional, and organizational development.* San Francisco, CA: Jossey-Bass.

Gappa, J. M., Austin, A. E., & Trice, A. G. (2007). *Rethinking faculty work: Higher education's strategic imperative.* San Francisco, CA: Jossey-Bass.

Ginsberg, M. B., & Wlodkowski, R. J. (2009). *Diversity and motivation: Culturally responsive teaching in college.* Minneapolis, MN: Wiley.

Henderson, C., Beach, A., & Finkelstein, N. (2011). Facilitating change in undergraduate STEM instructional practices: An analytic review of the literature. *Journal of Research in Science Teaching, 48*(8), 952–984.

Hines, S. R. (2009). Investigating faculty development program assessment practices: What's being done and how can it be improved? *Journal of Faculty Development, 23*(3), 5–19.

Ho, A., Watkins, D., & Kelly, M. (2001). The conceptual change approach to improving teaching and learning: An evaluation of a Hong Kong staff development programme. *Higher Education, 42*(2), 143–169.

Hurney, C. A., Harris, N. L., Prins, S. C. B., & Kruck, S. E. (2014). The impact of a learner-centered, mid-semester course evaluation on students. *Journal of Faculty Development, 28*(3), 55–62.

Hutchings, P. (2010). *Opening doors to faculty involvement in assessment.* Urbana: University of Illinois and Indiana University, National Institute for Learning Outcomes Assessment.

Johnson, W. B. (2007). *On being a mentor: A guide for higher education faculty.* Mahwah, NJ: Erlbaum.

Kern, B., Mettetal, G., Dixson, M., & Morgan, R. K. (2015). The role of SoTL in the academy: Upon the 25th anniversary of Boyer's *Scholarship Reconsidered. Journal of the Scholarship of Teaching and Learning, 15*(3), 1–14.

Kezar, A. (2012). *Embracing non-tenure track faculty: Changing campuses for the new faculty majority.* New York, NY: Routledge.

Kezar, A., & Sam, C. (2010). *Understanding the new majority of non-tenure-track faculty in higher education: Demographics, experiences, and plans of action.* San Francisco, CA: Jossey-Bass.

Kober, N. (2015). *Reaching students: What research says about effective instruction in undergraduate science and engineering.* Washington, DC: National Academy of Sciences.

Kuscera, J. V., & Svinicki, M. (2010). Rigorous evaluations of faculty development programs. *Journal of Faculty Development, 24*(2), 5–18.

Lee, V. S. (2010). Program types and prototypes. In K. H. Gillespie & D. L. Robertson (Eds.), *A guide to faculty development* (pp. 21–33). San Francisco, CA: Jossey-Bass.

Little, D. (2014). Reflections on the state of the scholarship of educational development. *To Improve the Academy, 33*(1), 1–13.

Mack, D., Watson, E. D., & Camacho, M. M. (Eds.). (2012). *Mentoring faculty of color: Essays on professional development and advancement in colleges and universities.* Jefferson, NC: McFarland.

Marbach-Ad, G., Egan, L. C., & Thompson, K. V. (Eds.). (2015). *A discipline-based teaching and learning center: A model for professional development.* London, UK: Springer.

Mårtensson, K., Roxå, T., & Olsson, T. (2011). Developing a quality culture through the scholarship of teaching and learning. *Higher Education Research & Development, 30*(1), 51–62.

Maxey, D., & Kezar, A. (2015). Revealing opportunities and obstacles for changing non-tenure-track faculty practices: An examination of stakeholders' awareness of institutional contradictions. *Journal of Higher Education, 86*(4), 564–594.

McDonald, J. (2010). Charting pathways into the field of educational development. *New Directions for Teaching and Learning, 122,* 37–45.

McShannon, J., & Hynes, P. (2005). Student achievement and retention: Can professional development programs help faculty GRASP it? *Journal of Faculty Development, 20*(2), 87–93.

Mellow, G. O., Woolis, D. D., Kalges-Bombich, M., & Restler, S. G. (2015). *Taking college teaching seriously: Pedagogy matters!* Sterling, VA: Stylus.

Menges, R. J., & Brinko, K. T. (1986). *Effects of student evaluation feedback: A meta-analysis of higher education research.* Paper presented at the Annual Meeting of the American Educational Research Association, San Francisco, CA.

Nasmith, L., & Steinert, Y. (2001). The evaluation of a workshop to promote interactive lecturing. *Teaching and Learning in Medicine, 13*(1), 43–48.

National Commission on Excellence in Education. (1983). *A nation at risk.* Washington, DC: Author.

Nelsen, W. C. (1981). *Renewal of the teacher-scholar: Faculty development in the liberal arts college.* Washington, DC: Association of American Colleges.

Olson, S., & Riordan, D. G. (2012). *Engage to excel: Producing one million additional college graduates with degrees in science, technology, engineering, and mathematics.* Retrieved from files.eric.ed.gov/fulltext/ED541511.pdf

POD Network. (n.d.). *5-year strategic plan*. Retrieved from podnetwork.org/content/uploads/Strategic-Plan13-18.pdf

Reder, M. (Ed). (2014). Supporting teaching and learning at small colleges—Past, present & future. *Journal on Centers for Teaching and Learning, 6*, 1–11.

Rice, R. E., Sorcinelli, M. D., & Austin, A. E. (2000). *Heeding new voices: Academic careers for a new generation*. Washington, DC: American Association of Higher Education.

Roxå, T., Mårtensson, K., & Cox, M. (2005). What initiates and enables becoming a scholarly teacher and SoTL?

Schroeder, C. M., & Associates (2010). *Coming in from the margins: Faculty development's emerging organizational development role in institutional change*. Sterling, VA: Stylus.

Schuster, J. H., & Finkelstein, M. J. (2006). *American faculty: The restructuring of academic work and careers*. Baltimore, MD: Johns Hopkins University Press.

Selingo, J. J. (2013). *College (un)bound: The future of higher education and what it means for students*. Boston, MA: Houghton Mifflin Harcourt.

Singer, S. R., Nielsen, N. R., & Schweingruber, H. A. (Eds.). (2012). *Discipline-based education research: Understanding and improving learning in undergraduate science and engineering*. Washington, DC: National Academies Press.

Slakey, L., & Gobstein, H. (2015). Toward a new normal. In G. C. Weaver, W. D. Burgess, A. L. Childress, & L. Slakey (Eds.), *Transforming institutions: Undergraduate STEM education for the 21st century* (pp. 485–496). West Lafayette, IN: Purdue University Press.

Sorcinelli, M. D., Austin, A. E., Eddy, P. L., & Beach, A. L. (2006). *Creating the future of faculty development: Learning from the past, understanding the present*. Bolton, MA: Anker.

Sorcinelli, M. D., & Ellozy, A. (in press). A history of faculty development: Combining research and professional wisdom. In C. Smith & K. Hudson (Eds.), *Faculty development in developing countries: Improving teacher quality in higher education*. New York, NY: Routledge/Taylor & Francis Group.

Sorcinelli, M. D., & Garner, A. (2013). Contributions to quality enhancement in the United States. In R. Land & G. Gordon (Eds.), *Enhancing quality in higher education: International studies in higher education* (pp. 94–105). London, UK: Routledge International.

Sorcinelli, M. D., Gray, T., & Birch, A. J. (2011). Faculty development beyond instructional development: Ideas centers can use. *To Improve the Academy, 30*, 247–261.

Steele, C. M. (2011). *Whistling Vivaldi: How stereotypes affect us and what we can do (issues of our time)*. New York, NY: Norton.

STEM Central. (n.d.). *Welcome*. Retrieved from stem-central.net

Trigwell, K. (2012). Evaluating the impact of university teaching development programmes. Methodologies that ask why there is an impact. In E. Simon & G. Pleschova (Eds.), *Teacher development in higher education: Existing programmes, programme impact, and future trends* (pp. 257–273). New York, NY: Routledge.

Trower, C. A. (2012). *Success on the tenure track: Five keys to faculty job satisfaction.* Baltimore, MD: John Hopkins University Press.

U.S. Department of Education, National Center for Education Statistics. (2014). *Table 315.10. Number of faculty in degree-granting postsecondary institutions, by employment status, sex, control, and level of institution: Selected years, fall 1970 through fall 2013.* Retrieved from nces.ed.gov/programs/digest/d14/tables/dt14_315.10.asp

Van Ummersen, C. A., McLaughlin, J. M., & Duranleau, L. J. (Eds.). (2014). *Faculty retirement: Best practices for navigating the transition.* Sterling, VA: Stylus.

Wehlburg, C. M. (2010). Assessment practices related to student learning. In K. H. Gillespie & D. L. Robertson (Eds.), *A guide to faculty development* (pp. 169–184). San Francisco, CA: Jossey-Bass.

Wieman, C., Perkins, K., & Gilbert, S. (2010). Transforming science education at large research universities: A case study in progress. *Change, 42*(2), 6–14.

Winkelmes, M. (Ed.). (2011). *Analysis of several themes emerging from the 2010 membership survey data.* Retrieved from docs.google.com/file/d/0B6yUeY3EibR9b0ZYOWZBaVlBamc/edit

Wright, D. L. (2002). Program types and prototypes. In K. H. Gillespie, L. R. Hilsen, & E. C. Wadsworth (Eds.), *A guide to faculty development: Practical advice, examples, and resources* (pp. 24–34). Bolton, MA: Anker.

Yakoboski, P. J. (2015, June). *Understanding the faculty retirement (non)decision.* Retrieved from www.tiaainstitute.org/public/pdf/understanding-the-faculty-retirement-nondecision.pdf

Yun, J. H., Baldi, B., & Sorcinelli, M. D. (2016). Mutual mentoring for early-career and underrepresented faculty: Model, research, and practice. *Innovative Higher Education, 4*(11), 1–11.

ABOUT THE AUTHORS

Andrea L. Beach is a professor of higher education leadership and codirector of the Center for Research on Instructional Change in Postsecondary Education at Western Michigan University. She founded and was director of the Office of Faculty Development at Western Michigan from 2008 to 2015. She received her MA in 1998 in adult and continuing education and her PhD in higher, adult, and lifelong education from Michigan State University in 2003. Her research centers on organizational change in higher education, support of innovation in teaching and learning, faculty learning communities, and faculty development as a change lever. She has been principal investigator and coprincipal investigator on several studies funded by the National Science Foundation focused on instructional change strategies that have produced articles and book chapters on instructional change strategies as well as instruments to self-report instruction and academic department climate for instructional improvement. She is director of a $3.2 million U.S. Department of Education First in the World project to undertake, document, and measure outcomes of institutional transformation aimed at improving the persistence and academic success of students from low-income backgrounds.

Mary Deane Sorcinelli is the Inaugural Distinguished Scholar in Residence at the Weissman Center for Leadership at Mount Holyoke College and a senior scholar at Bay View Alliance for the Reform of STEM (science, technology, engineering, and mathematics) Undergraduate Education. She previously served as associate provost and was founding director of the Center for Teaching & Faculty Development, professor of educational policy at the University of Massachusetts Amherst (1988–2014), and director of the Office of Faculty Development at Indiana University Bloomington (1983–1988). She is a well-known researcher in the areas of professional development of faculty across all career stages, mentoring, learner-centered teaching, improvement of teaching and learning in higher education, and the role of teaching centers in fostering twenty-first-century faculty learning. She has directed a number of externally grant-funded projects aimed at promoting educational innovations. In 2006 she was honored with the Bob Pierleoni Spirit of POD Award for outstanding lifetime achievement and leadership in the enhancement of teaching, learning, and faculty development. She also served as president/executive board member of the POD Network from 2000 to 2004 and Senior Scholar of the American Association for Higher Education.

Sorcinelli has provided faculty development teaching and consultations in international settings that include Canada, China, Egypt, England, Germany, Greece, Ireland, Puerto Rico, Saudi Arabia, and Taiwan. She visited the American University in Cairo, Egypt, as a distinguished visiting professor and was awarded a Whiting Foundation Fellowship to the National University of Ireland Galway. She holds an MA in English from Mount Holyoke College and an EdD in educational policy from University of Massachusetts Amherst.

Ann E. Austin is professor of higher, adult, and lifelong education at Michigan State University, where she twice has held the Mildred B. Erickson Distinguished Chair, from 2005 to 2008 and in 2014. She took a leave in 2015. She is now serving as a program director in the Division of Undergraduate Education at the National Science Foundation. Her research concerns faculty careers and professional development; teaching and learning in higher education; the academic workplace; organizational change; doctoral education; and reform in science, technology, engineering, and mathematics (STEM) education. She is a fellow of the American Educational Research Association, is past president of the Association for the Study of Higher Education, and was a Fulbright fellow in South Africa in 1998. She is a founding coleader of the Center for the Integration of Research, Teaching, and Learning and was the principal investigator of study funded by the National Science Foundation on organizational change strategies that support the success of women scholars in STEM fields. Her work is widely published, including *Educating Integrated Professionals: Theory and Practice on Preparation for the Professoriate* (Jossey-Bass, 2008), *Rethinking Faculty Work: Higher Education's Strategic Imperative* (Jossey-Bass, 2007), *Creating the Future of Faculty Development: Learning From the Past, Understanding the Present* (Jossey-Bass, 2006), and *Developing New and Junior Faculty* (Jossey-Bass, 1992), as well as other books, articles, chapters, and monographs concerning faculty issues and other higher education topics in the United States and in international contexts. She served as a member of the study team for the Asian Development Bank's project and monograph series on Higher Education in Dynamic Asia. She has worked with colleagues at the national and institutional levels on higher education issues in a number of countries, including Australia, China, Egypt, Finland, India, Malaysia, Oman, the Philippines, South Africa, Thailand, the United Arab Emirates, and Vietnam.

Jaclyn K. Rivard is a PhD student in organizational leadership, policy, and development at the University of Minnesota. With a focus on higher education, her research interests include equity and access, policy, civic engagement, and faculty development. She holds an MA from Western Michigan University in educational leadership, research, and technology with a focus on higher education and student affairs. While a student at Western Michigan, she worked in the Office of Faculty Development as a graduate assistant with new faculty seminar, faculty learning communities, faculty development workshops, and research in faculty development. During this time she also held internships in the Graduate College and the College of Arts and Sciences Advising Office. Her BA is in political science with a minor in women's studies from the University of Wisconsin–Superior. While a student there, she worked as a research assistant in assessment, provided research support for *By the Ore Docks: A Working People's History of Duluth* (University of Minnesota Press, 2006), and held internships with Congressman James Oberstar and the Human Rights Campaign. She previously worked as a program director for the Girl Scouts of the United States of America, where she focused heavily on community engagement, and served on a national committee focused on engaging girls in the fields of science, technology, engineering, and mathematics.

Taking College Teaching Seriously: Pedagogy Matters! breaks new ground in professional development. Each faculty member is at the center of the learning experience, stimulated and supported by peers working in similar contexts. They share a desire to see more students learn deeply and find that honing their skill at adapting to the learning needs of specific classes and students allows them to realize this goal. This book illuminates the link between faculty teaching expertise and improving student outcomes.

22883 Quicksilver Drive
Sterling, VA 20166-2102   Subscribe to our e-mail alerts: www.Styluspub.com

Also available from Stylus

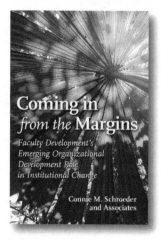

Coming in from the Margins
Faculty Development's Emerging Organizational Development Role in Institutional Change

Connie Schroeder

With Phyllis Blumberg, Nancy Van Note Chism, Catherine E. Frerichs, Susan Gano-Phillips, Devorah Lieberman, Diana G. Pace, and Tamara Rosier

"This book raises the level of discussion about the valuable role that teaching and learner centers [TLCs], their directors, and faculty developers can have in transforming student learning. The book comes at a time when we have reached a crossroads in the role of the TLC and its director. No longer can the TLC be marginalized if an institution wants to be responsive to calls for academic reforms or new strategic directions. TLCs can be the key facilitators that bring different stakeholders together to strategize and collaborate on an organizational level while still fulfilling their traditional roles of supporting and developing the capacity of individual faculty members. *Coming in from the Margins* should be read by faculty developers and by all leaders in higher education involved in collaborative and cross-functional initiatives relating to student learning and institutional assessments."—*The Review of Higher Education*

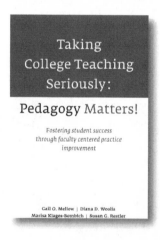

Taking College Teaching Seriously: Pedagogy Matters!
Fostering Student Success Through Faculty-Centered Practice Improvement

Gail O. Mellow, Diana D. Woolis, Marisa Klages-Bombich, and Susan Restler

Foreword by Rosemary Arca

This book presents a model of embedded professional development, which capitalizes on the affordances of technology to enable groups of faculty to examine their practice in a non-evaluative context but with a clear focus on improvement. The core of the work involves individual reflection and the design provides for an accessible way to "see" into the classrooms of discipline peers. Most importantly, the *Taking College Teaching Seriously!* experience is not an intense one-shot, but rather a structured opportunity for a faculty member to examine and adapt practice over time and to assess the impact of changes on student learning.